CONTENTS

Acknowledgements

Thank you to Pen to Print for providing inspirational courses that encourage and enable success in getting work published.

Thanks to Claire Buss for all her help in assisting me to understand how to publish this work on Amazon.

Thanks to Mary Walsh for her encouragement and proofreading.

Thanks also to Joseph Beckett, Adrian Ward and Amy Thellasson for proofreading.

Thanks to Philomena Chipman for listening and for her help.

I thank God for His care, provision, and protection throughout my travels.

My intention is that His goodness is not forgotten, or overlooked, during that time of my life.

I want to share my experiences, and this book is part one in the series of my diary and letters and I hope to follow up with the rest of my travels soon.

INTRODUCTION

Whilst sorting out my cupboard, I came across a diary, and a bundle of letters, that I had written over 50 years ago, together with film slides, which were a bit faded with age. The thought crossed my mind that, when I die, they might easily be thrown out, and no one would know their story. So, I decided to type them up, and made a book, for a bit of family history of' Granny's Adventures."

In 1966 I travelled overland to India on a bus. Then, alone, on to Australia and New Zealand, where I worked. On the route home, I visited missionaries in a few countries and ended up going across Russia on the Trans-Siberian Railway.

I want to preserve these, my first impressions, for future generations. They reflect that period of the 1960s, and how it was, then, travelling overland, meeting unfamiliar people, seeing new places, and experiencing their customs.

The world has changed a lot since then. My journal is a glimpse back to a past time of freedom when "over landers" went on adventures. This journey is probably impossible now. Trouble began with the six-day war between Jordan and Israel in 1967. This was followed by unrest across Syria, Iraq, Iran, and Afghanistan.

When I eventually returned home, I was invited to numerous places to show my slides and tell my stories. People loved them and I was in great demand. Now I am inviting you to share my journey.

Overland travel from London to India was popular in the 1950s and 1960s. In the 1960s, people went by car, land rovers or bus. There were two bus companies, Indiaman, and Penn Overland. I went with Penn. It was advertised as a luxury bus with a toilet and air conditioning, but unfortunately, neither was available on the bus we had. The journey took nine weeks from London to Bombay. We stopped every night, and every four days we stayed for two nights.

People who travelled this route with me were ordinary people, many of whom sailed on from Bombay to Australia and New Zealand, or back to England. We were young and old, professional people of all kinds. We were known as the Over landers. In the 1970s, people who travelled a similar route, but to Kathmandu, were a different group of people, known as Hippies. They went there to buy drugs, so it became known as the Hippie Route.

It has been said that no one can go on a journey and come back quite the same. That is true. A journey of this kind incorporates so many themes that people feel passionate about. History, art, culture and religion, customs, education, health, and hygiene. All are glimpsed in this book. Travel does broaden the mind. In fact, I was so influenced by what I had seen and learnt that when I returned home, I trained to be a teacher, and taught in multicultural schools. So, it changed my life.

"Comes not back to man again the past life, or the neglected opportunity."

STARTING OFF

For several years I expressed a burning desire to go round the world. I wanted to see how people in other countries lived. Overland was my choice. The idea became an obsession. I had considered going alone on my Lambretta scooter, so contacted the Automobile Association for a route. They informed me that there was no made road across the desert. That reassured my father, who had been in Iraq in the forces, in World War One, and knew what the terrain was like. My family was very concerned, so I decided that I would have to forget it or go another way.

One day my opportunity came. My cousin Joan suggested that we went to Cooks Travel Agents in London to enquire if there were any alternative methods of travel. They confirmed that neither made-up roads, nor trains, crossed the desert, so air or ship were the only choices left. That was not what I wanted because I wanted to see the countries for myself and find out how other people lived. Their customs, costumes and scenery were what I wanted to see. I knew that I didn't really have enough money, and any travel would have to be on a shoestring, and I would have to work my passage home.

As we came out of Cooks, Joan shouted, "Look, that's what you want!" There, across the road, was a bus parked, and written on its side was, "Penn Tours. Journey of a Lifetime. Overland to India."

I wrote down the phone number and phoned a couple of days later. There was one place left. It was leaving in three weeks' time. I booked and was ready for the "off."

My employer, the Civil Service, needed four weeks' notice, but fortunately, they accepted three in the unusual circumstances. The cost of the bus ticket was £145 for nine weeks, travel only, from London to Bombay.

The news got around, and The Ilford Recorder came to the house and took a photo. I was on the front page, the lead story!

"GIRL'S DATE IN PERSIAN DESERT"

"An Ilford girl, who will be off on a round-the-world trip next week, plans to meet a girlfriend on the route, in the middle of the Persian desert. Elizabeth Freeman, 25, has been "plucking up the courage" to go off on her own for eight years. Next Saturday she will set off with a party aboard a bus and travel across Europe, through Greece, the Holy Land, then on to the Middle East, and from there to Bombay, India.

"This is the part of the trip that I'm not looking forward to. I didn't want to go with a party by bus, I originally wanted to go entirely on my own by motor scooter. But I just had to take the opportunity to go, and it meant by bus."

The bus will be travelling via Persia. Her friend Clair Smith is teaching there.

"I thought that as I would be passing through, we could meet up. We have arranged to see each other in the desert on October 28".

Once she arrives in India, Elizabeth's solo route will include Australia, New Zealand, Japan, then back across Russia on the Trans-Siberian Railway.

"I'm a little bit scared of doing this on my own. People have told me such horrible stories about what could happen, but I have been wanting to go round the world for eight years. I won't settle down until I have been."

She reckons to be home in July, when she plans to set off again with Clair Smith to visit Canada and America. Elizabeth went to Iceland on her own last year.

"I don't feel that I am on my own because one meets people and makes friends. I'll be able to please myself and see what I want to see by going alone."

I remember the excitement of everyone. A neighbour said, "Don't forget toilet rolls." So, the night before I left, she came round and helped with unrolling toilet rolls and folding them to pack flat.

WEEK ONE

Day 1   24th September

LONDON TO OSTEND, BELGIUM

The bus left Mayfair Place, London, early the following morning, 24th September. I was surprised, but pleased, to see several of my friends there, to join my parents and cousin Joan, to wave me off. A friendly girl indicated to me to sit beside her. We sat together throughout the entire journey to Bombay.

It was coming into Autumn. I enjoyed the ride and the colour of trees on the way. At Dover, there was mist over the sea. We left this bus in England and took our luggage onto the boat, as our proper bus was waiting for us in Belgium. Every day we all moved one seat round, so that everyone had the experience of every seat, and consequently the front seat, which made it fair.

Although the bus was supposed to be a luxury bus with air conditioning, our air conditioning never worked, and there was no toilet. So, when we got to remote areas, like the desert, we had "Bush Stops," which were men to the left and women to the right of the bus.

Sadly, the first seven days' diary, containing details of some of my fellow travellers, was lost. I might have posted it in a bin instead of a post box because letterboxes are different in every country. Letters home, tell the story of those days.

Dear Mum and Dad, after leaving you in **London**, we went to **Dover** and got on the boat at 10.30 am, but it didn't go until 1 pm, so Gill and I enjoyed ourselves watching people. The boat was overcrowded.

There were old dears wrapped up warmly in deck chairs. Porters shouted and flew about the place, causing pandemonium, calling out the numbers of cases for people to go and collect. As people piled onto the boat, the gangways began to lower, with the tide.

When we got on, we had a steep climb up the gangplank, but by the time we were ready to go, people were walking down the gangplank onto the boat.

Women anxiously watched for their bags to arrive, convinced that they were lost. It sounded like a fish auction at the market. While all this was going on, another trainload of people arrived. The deckchair men ran around, all the more, in ever-decreasing circles, banging chairs, tripping over cases, bumping into people, and shouting in French and English.

A holiday party of North country women arrived, and they were terrified of being split up, so collected as many chairs as they could, and put them all together with bags on some, and sitting on others, chatting together in loud voices, yelling out, "Have you seen so and so?" "Where's so and so?", "No, you can't sit here this chair is saved." They were right beside me and succeeded in moving me along, and all my baggage, to make room for yet another of their party.

Eventually, we cast off. As we sailed out of Dover harbour the sun shone brightly on us and sparkled on the water. Leaving the white cliffs of Dover behind, we sat back to enjoy the warmth of the sun and the journey ahead. There were a remarkable number of boats about, so plenty to watch.

It wasn't long, however, before this peaceful state was broken, for the courier had advised us to change some currency on board. When we went down to do this there was a queue of about thirty people before us, and we had to stand down in the dark, hot hole of the ship for one and a half hours.

This was entertaining. It's surprising how people hate queue jumpers and tell them so. There were fussy old women in this queue who told Gill and me, "You know you are behind us," because we happened to be leaning on the only available wall space, which was just ahead of them.

The same thing happened in other queues nearby, for the restaurant and snack bar. I stood and listened. People were constantly asking me; which queue was which. Finally, we emerged out into the sun and my seat hadn't been taken!

Then something most surprising happened. Just guess? The boat broke down! It was unbelievable. When it started up again it travelled very slowly indeed, so we docked at 5.15 pm instead of at 4 pm.

Everyone getting off the boat, was even worse than getting on. Some waved and called to people on the pier who had come to meet them. Others fought frantically, to get off first. People that had looked ladylike on the boat journey now behaved like mad women, and city gent types of men turned into stampeding hooligans.

I stood back out of the way and let them all off. I wasn't going to be torn in half, so I eventually stepped off at leisure. As they battled off, I saw one old lady, who had got wise with age, for when the baggage porter was pushing past everyone with a case slung by a strap over each shoulder, she got right behind him and followed him through, with no trouble at all.

The customs hall had cleared of people, and cases, while we still waited. An official asked us where we were going, to see if he could find them. He was taken aback when we said, "India," and told us to get in the coach and they would come. They did, but something had happened to my small case, because it was scratched and marked and had a small tear, so I was glad I hadn't left my tape recorder in it.

It was fine in Ostend. Our bus seats tipped back and had roof windows that opened. Due to arriving late, we stayed the first night in a hotel in Ostend, and a good job too, for by the time we got our cases off, there wasn't time to go anywhere else, due to the fact that as our cases went on first, they came off last.

Roger, the guide, on this first day, reminded us that we were not tourists, but travellers throughout this trip. "There is a vast difference between the two. A tourist travels luxuriously and can stop when and where he likes, but we are all travellers together and our destination is India, which is a long way away. Consequently, we must consider each other throughout the trip and must not hold up everyone else by being late back to the coach, nor expect the driver to keep stopping for individuals to take photographs."
This, we all appreciated.
"We will stop each night in a town where there is ample accommodation of all sorts to meet everyone's

requirements, and we will also stop for lunch, and morning and afternoon tea."

The thought of tea breaks or chi stops as they were eventually called, cheered my spirits immensely.

Roger went on to explain that every four days we would have a free day for sightseeing in a place of interest.

"Now, as travellers together we must think of the smooth running of the trip, so we will not unload all our luggage every night because this will give the driver a lot of hard work during the nine weeks' journey. Instead, we will keep inside the bus just our overnight baggage and will keep the rest of our luggage locked away in the boot."

This seemed reasonable to me, and as we had only been permitted to take one overnight bag and one 26" case with us this did not cause any hardship. I had managed to sneak an extra little bag that contained a small tape recorder. I was glad to have this with me, for many times during the journey I tape-recorded sounds that were unfamiliar in England, such as Muslims being called to prayer from the mosque minarets, national music, and native market sounds.

As I looked at all my travelling companions during this first dinner time, I wondered what type of people they were, what had made them all come on such a venture. There were several types of people in our group. Some wanted to travel comfortably and could afford good accommodation. These, we nicknamed the Capitalists. Then there were the rest of us younger ones who were travelling on a shoestring and were prepared to rough it, so we travelled cheap- cheap.

The age range went from 21 to 84. In fact, a sturdy 84-year-old managed to outstrip us all many a time in the hot countries, for he was really tough. He and his younger wife owned a dairy farm in New Zealand, and they had been back to visit England, or rather, "The Old Country of their Ancestors," as they preferred to say.

There were forty-five of us altogether, to start with, although we lost a few on the route. Most people were either from Australia and New Zealand and were returning home overland, to add variety, as they had gone out by boat to visit England and the continent. Several of them were nurses and teachers. Gill Pardoe, who was a nurse, planned to catch a ship back to England from Bombay.

There were eight of us who soon palled up together, mainly because of accommodation and economy. Besides Gill, there was Dorothy Spendlove, from Australia, and Susanna Quin, an Australian nurse.

Martin was a Danish- New Zealand farm-lad of 21. Malcolm Cameron was a pleasant New Zealander in his early twenties. He had a sensitive, kindly nature, and was creative. He was of slight, elfin build, and agile. He was a teacher and had just spent a year teaching boys aged from eleven to fourteen, in northern England. Physical education was one of the subjects he taught.

Barry Gray, who was a mystery from England, was a caring pleasant person. We were convinced that he was from the aristocracy because he never had to work, had his own money, dressed in decent quality clothing, and spoke well Bob Handley was an older, quiet Australian who joined in with our group occasionally.

There were single ladies in their forties and fifties. One lady was English, but she worked in a home for children in Australia. Another lady from Yorkshire turned out to be quite a merry sort who kept us amused, at times, by singing funny little ditties and songs.

No one guessed at this stage that our driver, Frank, would get engaged to one of the group, halfway through the venture, but there you are, love is to be found wherever you look. As I looked at all my travelling companions, I knew that I was going to enjoy this trip and was going to be happy, and this turned out to be quite right.

After dinner some of us walked through the streets of Ostend, which were all lit and decorated with fairy lights, to have a last glimpse of the sea. I felt quite nostalgic to think that I would not see the sea again until Istanbul, because I love the sea.

Perhaps I would have felt quite differently had the crossing been rough enough to make us all seasick, but instead, it had been a calm journey, like a millpond, so such an enjoyable trip across the Channel.

That first night seven of us shared a room, and three of us slept together in one bed.

Day 2   25th September

OSTEND TO PARIS

The next day we took the coast road to France and then inland across flat country, where there were lots of drainage dykes.

We reached Paris at lunchtime, so had a half-day to look around. I walked with Annett. We went beside the River Seine and saw many booksellers. Then to the Notre Dame where men were collecting money outside.

Many arty people were painting and selling work. I always loved Paris, not that I have visited it many times, it is so interesting and seems to have a romantic fairyland charm about it. I think this is because the buildings are so beautifully floodlit at night.

Annett was plump, young-looking, aged between thirty to thirty-five. She was pleasant, and always thought carefully before speaking.

We sat chatting outside a café, drinking coffee, right beside a large grating which led down to the Metro.

Suddenly she was filled with ecstasy as she cried,

"Oh, What a lovely smell. I love the smell of the Metros. It reminds me of when I used to live in Paris." To me, it smelt like a laundry, but to Annett, it was one of the best smells in this world. She knew Paris very well having lived there for a time, and she walked us back to our hotel, past the flat where she used to live.

She came from London and was interested in Antiques and said,

"What about you and I going into partnership, in London, and having an Antique shop in Chelsea?"

Somehow, I didn't think it would be a very fair partnership if she had all the money and I had none to put down!!

Eventually, we arrived back at our little hotel which we called the Flea Pit.

Day 3   26th September

PARIS TO PONTARLIER FRANCE

We picked up one more person for the bus, then travelled a long day across France to **Pontarlier**. The scenery changed a lot and became more interesting as we went south towards the Alps. The weather was beautiful and sunny in the morning. On route, we stopped at Sens to look inside Saint Etienne Cathedral, which is Gothic and building started in 1122. It has beautiful stained glass windows, including a Rose window, where Gospel parables are depicted. Its pillars and double columns give a strong appearance. It is steeped in history.

When at last we reached Pontarlier, most of our party stayed in an old rambling coaching inn. We discovered that the Youth Hostel was closed. So four of us scouted around and found a cheap, backstreet hotel. The woman only charged us 4/- for the night because we were YHA members. and shared a room, above the pub, with two beds. Dorothy had a handy little electric element, that she had bought in Germany, which boiled a cup of water. So we were able to spend the evening chatting and drinking tea.

Dorothy was a young auburn-haired Jewish girl, who became a great companion of mine. She had had a nose operation whilst in England, but despite this, our driver warned her to take exceptional care in Jerusalem, which then still belonged to the Arabs.

Day 4   27th September

PONTARLIER TO ST. CHRISTOPH, ITALY

Post Card picture of Vallorbe frontier France Switzerland. "Today dawned a misty morning, shrouding the autumn leaves, but later on, as the mist went, it turned into a beautiful sunny day. Soon we were at the foothills of the Alps with attractive rolling hills. The scenery was magnificent. Now we are at the Swiss frontier and will pass through Switzerland to Italy to stay at **Aosta** tonight."

At the frontier into **Switzerland**, we changed a little currency, because our destination that night was Italy, so we only required a small amount of Swiss money, not more than a pound, between two of us, at the most.

It was not long before we came to Lake Geneva which was overhung by mist and surrounded by terraced hills. Vines with clusters of lush grapes grew.

The bus stopped for a while. Some people were water skiing and there was a Bible kiosk at the water's edge. It was very warm.

Then climbing up over the St Bernard Pass, we went through the new St Bernard Tunnel, which had only been opened in March 1964, and we came to the Italian border, which was in the tunnel.

At last, we arrived at **Aosta**, Italy, an industrial town set in a valley, and we stayed just outside in the village of **St Christophe.**

This Alpine village looked beautiful in the evening sun. People were still working in the vineyard. Clusters of grapes hung over terraced walls, and walnuts grew by the road. As we walked up to the little church on the hill, we could hear the deep tone of cowbells ringing as the animals were being gathered in. Their cheerful clanging sound echoed around the valley.

The graveyard was tiered, quite different from any found in England. Graves were similar to boxes set into the wall, like tombs. I became intrigued by the variety in styles, of cemeteries, throughout the world.

Most people stayed in the hotel, they were the "capitalists," but fourteen of us girls, the "peasants", slept outside, under the stars, in sleeping bags, on camp beds. Talk about a laugh, there was the traffic rushing by on the main road, and one girl was changing into her nightclothes. I slept with my clothes on to keep nicely warm. Just after we had all got into bed, two of the Italian customs officials arrived at the hotel, "To see the girls," they said. Cheeky!

Day 5   28th September

ST. CHRISTOPH TO VENICE ITALY

This morning we were rudely awakened, at 6.25 am, by a dog barking at us. After sleeping all night in my clothes, it was pleasant to have a shower.

Breakfast consisted of one roll and coffee. As the hotel was unable to fill my flask with hot water, one of the boys kindly gave me his coffee to fill it.

The first hour, or so, of the journey, was interesting. The mountain road wound high up above the valley and the driver was blowing his horn at every bend. A stony riverbed lay in the valley below, with trickling streams wending their way along.

Houses, built closely together, had no clear layout, looking disarranged, as if fallen down in a shower of rain. Their large, grey slate rooves, gave them a certain charm and character.

Our bus took us through Aosta, which is surrounded by mountains. It was a modern-looking, industrial town with smoky factories, blocks of flats, and fast wide roads.

There were not many people about. I saw a man and woman sitting outside a restaurant with a drink. She looked bored and idle, gazing at the road junction and traffic. She had such a lost, lonely look in her eye I just could not forget her.

The scenery was uninspiring, conjuring up an atmosphere of desperation and loneliness. A little, old man was struggling along with a large sack on his back. Probably working to the end for existence, I thought. Two young men were repairing a road sign, and a group of military men marched down the road. Soon we were on the motorway to Venice, and the rest of the day's journey was dull and boring.

Coffee break and lunch break, both had to be taken at the motorway restaurants, so some of us sat on the grass and picnicked at lunchtime.

The scenery was very flat and monotonous, with occasional industrial towns in the distance. Gill and I amused ourselves, part of the afternoon, by reading poetry to each other and playing twenty questions.

The only real interest to the day's journey was when the coach broke down, due to a petrol leak. This was the second breakdown. The weather has been fine all the time, so far.

Eventually, we arrived in **Venice** at 4.45 pm, only to find that the water buses were on a two-day strike, which meant that we could not reach the Youth Hostel. So the driver welcomed us to his coach to sleep, because he regards this as his home, and felt as if he was offering us hospitality.

Before sleep, he took the five of us to a workmen's cafe, by the car park, where we had vegetable soup, spaghetti, fried fish, and coffee. Although it was only a work man's cafe the service was good, and it was marvellous to get a meal inside us. All the other meals, since Ostend, had been snacks.

Our beds were made up on the coach floor and we just fitted in nicely, although there was hardly room to turn over. Unfortunately, the engine was under the coach, so it was hot until it cooled down.The coach was parked down by the harbour. It was so beautiful to look out at the large ships with their lights reflecting into the moving water. It reminded me of Woolwich. There is something so fascinating, mysterious, and romantic about boats. I think it must be the thought of where they have been and where they are going.

Day 6   29th September

VENICE

This morning we awoke and packed our sleeping bags, and then made full use of the public facilities in the car park, where we were able to have a wash and freshen up, and this only cost 30 lire each, which wasn't bad. It was a treat to wear a dress again.

Today was our free day in Venice and it was quite fine, only a shower or two at times, but nothing to speak of. First, we made our way to the Piazza Roma and then crossed over a canal by a rounded bridge with wide steps on either side. Now I felt as if I was really in Venice.

Our first port of call was at a café, for cappuccino and croissant, it was delicious. Then we wandered around getting hopelessly lost. Even though we had a map, it didn't make any difference, we still got lost.

Venice was a fascinating place, with many waterways, bridges, and boats. Narrow streets and back alleys were only wide enough for two in places. Washing hung from windows. There was such a happy, carefree atmosphere with people singing and floating along in gondolas. Others were working hard. Shops competing to sell their wares. Markets were the places to find bargains. Venice was full of interest and excitement.

We were told that in Roman times, Venice was a swamp, then a home for refugees, and later a fishing town. By the time of the crusaders, she had a large navy. When the Roman Empire fell, she was dependent on trade with Constantinople, who used to hire her boats to sail to the Holy Land for crusades. Venice later declined until she became how she is now. Houses are built on piles, but in 1,000 years Venice sinks three meters. Venice inspired Shakespeare to write of her in "The Merchant of Venice."

We crossed the Rialto Bridge, with its little shops, and stood gazing down at the activity on the Grand Canal. Although the water buses were out of action there was still plenty to see. Barges sailing up and down, crammed full of standing passengers, these took the place of the buses.

Gondoliers merrily punted along, giving enjoyment to their passengers. Various boats were tied to coloured poles, like enlarged barbers' poles, and people sat eating and drinking at tables, beside the water. Others looked out of their windows across the canal.

We walked on and came to waterside restaurants with greenery climbing around the windows. They looked so enticing and romantic. Eventually, we came to St Mark's Square, with her countless pigeons. Every time the bells rang, or clocks struck, the birds all took off, like "knocking off time" at a factory. At 2 pm the bells really went to town and made such a beautiful, but deafening noise.

It was high tide and the water had risen into St Mark's Square, so planks of wood were set across to the steps of the Basilica of St Mark, for us to enter. Inside it was in the process of being cleaned, and where the work had been completed it was beautiful, with gilt pictures in abundance on the ceiling, and walls. The floor was an old mosaic that was worn down and uneven. Behind the altar was a Byzantine screen called the Gold Pala. This is a priceless piece of work consisting of over 2,400 precious stones inlaid in gold. There are alleged to be 1,300 pearls, 300 emeralds, 300 sapphires, 400 garnets, 100 amethysts, plus rubies and topazes. The golden pieces are made of a thin gold leaf laid between two layers of clear glass. Pictures, on beaten enamel, depicted the life of Christ. Beaten enamel work, so I was told, is now an extinct art, which, adds to the value of the work. A light was shining onto this which made it sparkle and shine splendidly.

Later we walked down to the main waterfront and saw a large white boat dock. It was the "Shalom," a Jewish boat full of Jewish Americans, who were on a cruise. Leaning on the rail of a bridge, we stood idly watching them disembark. Most of the people were elderly and well dressed and proudly walked off. I imagine that most of them were rich, but I couldn't see any that looked happy.

One couple was entertaining, the husband walked down the gangplank with open arms to embrace the whole of Venice, and his wife followed. He swept, round with a slight bow to her, and held out his hand. At the same time, the uniformed ship official also held out his hand to assist her, but she turned her back slightly to him and faced her husband, who took her by the arm and off they pranced.

Two women really amused me. They minced down the gangplank with very hesitant steps, obviously expecting a crew member to help them. They put on such an act of helplessness I could not help laughing, because anyone could have got down without any assistance at all. At last two members came to help and the women were all grins and smiles and happy again. As we walked along, we could not help overhearing conversations, but they all seemed aggressive and agitated towards each other.

On the way back we passed a wall, with an open doorway. Inside was a dim, half-covered, courtyard with plants creeping up the walls, and a stone staircase at one side, which was so typically Venetian. Death certificates were stuck on the walls. People have to be taken to the mainland for burial.

On our journey around we looked in a Greek Orthodox Church, with many paintings on the walls and ceiling, they were so dark we could not see much detail.

Soon we decided to buy food for the next day's journey, and this left me with 120 lire, so supper was out. Instead, I ate salami and bread with grapes. This left me with enough money for the next day for a wash and cheap coffee.

That night, when we got back into the bus, it started to rain with thunder and lightning, we just made it in time. We were very tired and slept at 9 p.m. very comfortably.

The driver has got off with one of the girls and we haven't been going a week yet.

Day 7   30th September

VENICE TO ZAGREB YUGOSLAVIA

This morning we awoke at 6.30 am and we cleaned out the coach. Rain was deluging down, and I got soaked walking the length of the bus, with an umbrella up, to empty the rubbish. When we were ready to wash the driver drove us over to the wash house. I stepped out, and offered to share my umbrella with him, he accepted, and as he did, I trod in a huge puddle that soaked his legs. I kept his head dry, and my feet got washed!!   He bought us all a cup of cappuccino, and we had a free wash because the lady wasn't there to take our money. I could, now, afford breakfast. Before, it was a toss-up between a small coffee and a wash.

We went to pick up the others, and as they were loading the cases a couple of us nipped off for espresso coffee and croissant. We drove through **Italy to the Yugoslav border**. Here we spent an hour for the lunch break. The customs official collected all our passports and handed them back with detachable visas. Here I changed some money.

We drove non-stop to Zagreb. The scenery was superb, with wide, fertile valleys, where meandering rivers wended their way along. Dotted over the valley were farmhouses, and deciduous trees radiant with autumn colours. As we passed along the road, even better views opened at every bend. There were deciduous forests of numerous shades of yellow, orange, red, rust, and green. On mountains, dense forests of fir trees grew, from which hung clusters of ripening cones.

Many humble dwellings had drying sheds, where tobacco was hung, in the summer. When we passed by, in autumn, yellow corn on the cob hung there decoratively. Yellow marrow grew at the edges of fields, and farmers ploughed their land with oxen, whilst others walked along with baskets scattering seed on the ground.

In communist countries, there appears to be equality amongst men and women. I passed a woman loading coal and others who were farming out on the fields with their children. Such happy family scenes. I was surprised to see Roman Catholic churches and wayside shrines in this communist land

We arrived at **Zagreb** at about 4.45 pm and stayed at a Motel, on the outskirts just through on the other side. Beryl, Annette, Dorothy, Gill, Suzanne, and I slept in a chalet for six, in the woodland. It was a novel triangular design, and great fun too.

The coach took a crowd of us to the supermarket to buy food, and it was as if we invaded the place, the poor shop assistants looked abashed. Eventually, I queued up to pay for my wares and found, to my embarrassment, that I had overspent and didn't have enough money to pay for everything, so I had a great unpacking session. I did not understand the currency because there were two in use, old and new currency, so I didn't bother to look at prices. To cap it all, when we got back, I found that I did have enough money, but had just got confused with it.

Whilst many of the others were dining high in the hotel, we gipsies ate our snack in the chalet. I had cold baked beans and sausage out of a tin, bread and milk, and the remains of my grapes. What a state to come to, but it tasted good. Later I had the immense pleasure of a hot shower and shampoo. How wonderful it felt. There we were, over in the wash house with other foreign campers, washing and scrubbing away, it was absolute bliss, and couldn't have been better if we'd paid the earth for it.   Our night's stay cost 1140 dinar.

At about 10 pm, Annette came in and, for fun, I put the tape recorder on, and then played it back to her It was such a laugh. She decided that she suddenly had to go to the loo but was afraid to cross the car park and wood to it, so I went with her, in my night attire, flowing hair and curlers, under a full moon. I must have looked like the madwoman from Hamlet. When we got back Annette was worried in case her bed was wet, and she got rheumatism, but we assured her she wouldn't. Then she got out her torch and had a good search for scorpions.

I liked this country very much. The autumn colours were incredibly beautiful on the swirly patterned hills. I'd like to go back there one day, for a camping holiday, as they have good facilities.

The motorway is called the Auto- put. It was built after Tito came into power and he got volunteers to build it. Farming is backward, but she produces more than she can eat, so exports some. Although it's a communist country, tipping is accepted.   Yugoslavia is more western than other communist countries because she had no aid from Russia when two million liberated themselves from communist power.

Popular foods here are stew and rice, meat, and vegetables.

WEEK TWO

Day 8   1st October

ZAGREB TO NIS

After breakfast, which was an event for me, was in the motel. We left Zagreb for Nis at 8 30 a.m.

The scenery was panoramic and beautiful. A wide openness. The valleys and rolling hills were ablaze with autumn colours.

Lunch break was taken at **Belgrade**, which is both ancient and modern. We stopped for an hour or so in the modern part, outside a restaurant, come superstore. We sat, like refugees, on stone seats outside the restaurant, carving up bread and meat, and I got covered in honey. Passers-by gave us the oddest of looks and not much wonder either.

Everything is controlled by the government and consequently, no one person is the owner of anything, and this tends to lead to a lack of responsibility and service. I visited the toilet there, but made a hasty retreat, deciding that I could wait, as it stunk, consisted of a "hit or miss" hole in the ground and was swarming with flies. In these conditions stood an old lady dressed in black, who was obviously the attendant, she was chattering to a young fellow who was sitting in the Ladies doing his homework!

The next move was to shop in the supermarket. After walking around twice, coming out, and then going in again, I, at last, discovered the food department. Here I stocked up because goods were supposed to be cheaper in Yugoslavia than in Greece. The queue for payment was tremendous, and everyone took their time, but at last, I was finished and out onto the bus.

From here we passed through old Belgrade, and amongst other things, saw the communist army barracks with its familiar red star over the gate.

The afternoon journey, through central Serbia to Nis, was long, and without a break, not even a breakdown! The scenery was attractive, and the setting sun was magnificent. It inspired me to write the following: -

> When the sun has shed its splendour
> And its heat upon the day,
> And the clouds begin to gather
> Round her beautiful last ray,
> When the mountains turn to darkness,
> And the mist begins to fall,
> Then I know my home is calling
> And must answer to its call.

It was dark by the time we reached **Nis** although only about 6.30 p.m. Nis was part of the Turkish Empire. In 1809 the Serbs from Nis rebelled against the Turks, but unsuccessfully, so their heads were chopped off and their skulls made into a Tower of Skulls. The Turks were good at this and often made such towers. The object was, to act as an example to any would-be rebels. Nis was the birthplace of Constantine the Great.

Roger, our guide, advised the girls not to go off anywhere alone, from then onwards for the whole of the trip. He told us that three years before the driver lost a girl in Beirut, and she was never seen since. He went to the British Consulate and everywhere, but she was never found. He was very worried.

On arrival at the motel some of us "refugee types" were billeted out in tents for two. I shared mine with

Gill. Some of the others had rooms for four which turned out to be chalets. The toilets and wash place here, again, were stinky and horrid, and so I didn't bother much about washing, but I did use it to wash my cabbage and carrots, which I had bought for tomorrow's meals.

This evening we splashed out and dined with the others, but the service was extremely slow. The place was crowded to capacity, and the tablecloths filthy. It was absolute shambles, with people trying to shout their orders at the waiter, above the thudding din of the band.

As well as this, no one really knew what they were ordering, and certainly couldn't pronounce it, so every time the waiter arrived at a table to take the order, someone had to jump up and dash round to find the menu at another table.

I tried to get a recording of the fast Slavonic music, but by the time I had got the recorder, the style of music had changed. We were convinced that the music was being played fast to make people gulp down their food and vacate the table quickly for the others waiting.

Dinner took about three hours to order, eat and pay for. Half that time was waiting to pay. This is because no one is personally responsible for the hotel and therefore waiters take their time.

After dinner, we were invited to see the chalet of four of the boys. So we eight sat chatting for quite a while. When eventually we got back to our tents, at about 11.30 p.m., we noticed how musty everything smelt, and the pillow was dirty and made us feel "cooty."

We were laying there gazing at the moonlight through the holes in the tent, when suddenly an Alsatian appeared at the tent door, followed by an

Austrian chap who invited us to go to a drinking party across the way, but we declined his invitation, as we thought it wasn't quite our cup of tea, especially at that time of night.

Day 9   2nd October

NIS YUGOSLAVIA TO THESSALONICA GREECE

This morning I was awakened at 5.30 a.m. by the dawn chorus. It was a confusion of noise that sounded like car wheels on wet roads, at first, until the harmony could be distinguished.

I was again awoken at 6 a.m. by hymn singing. It did sound good, so refreshing. It was a German party having a service.

After coffee for breakfast, for me, we left at 8 a.m. and called in to see the famous Tower of Skulls, at **Scheltema Yugoslavia.**

It was gruesome and creepy. The heads had been mounted in the mortar and allowed to rot and decay. I found it revolting to look at and couldn't get out of there quick enough!

The morning's journey took us past small houses with yellow corn on the cob hanging out on racks, and green and red peppers strung up by the doors. Tobacco still lay on racks drying from the summer.

Women worked hard in the fields, digging and minding cattle, whilst goats and sheep were led along their pastures by lonely-looking men. Tents were erected to make shelters for the sheep.

Lunch break was taken at **Skopje,** which is the capital of Macedonia. There is a large community of Muslims, near Skopje, and this was the first place where we heard people being called to prayer.

It is the place where an earthquake took place three years ago, and the railway station, which was once the best in Yugoslavia, has been left as a memorial to the earthquake. The clock stands at 5.15 a.m., the time the earthquake took place, and lumps of concrete hang pathetically from the ceiling on pieces of metal cord. Squalor and debris still lie roundabout.

It is indeed an incredibly sad and heart-rending sight. To complete this picture, of desperation, that the earthquake caused, are little, ragged, barefooted children, hopping amongst the debris begging. Their poverty-stricken-looking mothers, with babies in arms, walk from one person to another muttering, "Dena please, Dena." We chose this spot to eat our lunch.

Only that morning I thought how hard up I was because I was trying to go as cheap as I could, in order to save my money, to make it last out. I thought to myself earlier that day, "Fancy just eating bread and cheese."

Then I saw these people starving hungry, and when I went to eat my one piece of bread and cheese, it stuck in my throat, at the sight of these poor wretches.

I had thought that my small amount of food for lunch wouldn't keep me going, but when I saw these poor, sad, thin people, I felt rich, and guilty at having so much, and my meagre dinner suddenly seemed fit for a queen.

Modern flats have sprung up where once older buildings stood, and jerry huts still stand, that were put up after the quake, as refugee houses.

Day 10   3rd October

THESSALONICA TO DELPHI GREECE

Departure time was due to be 8 a.m. today, but the coach wouldn't go, and we eventually left at 10 a.m. In the meantime, I walked around with Anastasia Romanoff, who is a remarkably interesting person to talk to. She was born in Poland, but as a child was shipped to China, where she was educated and taught in the Russian language. Now she is resident in the USA and is married to a professor of Embryology, who lectures at a university, whilst she writes books, with him, on medical science. She told me about their work and gave me a poem her husband had written because he has had two or three poetry books published, also she told me about the Russian royal family and how they were killed.

The ride during the morning took us past Mount Olympus, which was capped with cloud, as is most usual. It was once believed to be the abode of the gods of ancient Greece. Passing through, what seemed to be, a never-ending, arid, sparsely vegetated landscape, I noticed wooden thatched shelters for sheep. They looked as if the slightest puff of wind would blow them over. Flocks of sheep picked amongst ploughed soil, often in very isolated places. Shepherds wearing typical shepherd's cloaks, and carrying crooks, watched over sheep, goats, or cows as they grazed. A couple of people watched animals grazing all day on next to nothing. I can't understand how they make a living

Houses looked dirty, dilapidated, and poor, with fences around the area, which were supposed to be gardens, but didn't manage to produce anything. One or two houses were well kept, clean, and brightly painted, and had flowers and vines creeping over porches. Through their open windows, I could see women, in black clothing, standing around, or sitting indoors chatting and entertaining each other. Here, in this part of **Greece,** cotton, and tobacco grow. The people are darker-skinned, and the written language is difficult to read.

When we reached the mountains, they really were something. Our coach spent half the day winding its way around hairpin bends and on unmade roads. The earth was red, and red dust had blown up onto the trees. When it was dark, we were still crossing the mountains, creepy, but worse for the driver, who I think did an excellent job.

Then we reached **Delphi,** a beautiful place, right up in the mountains, on Mount Parnassus, overlooking a valley to the sea, in the Gulf of Corinth. As I looked out of the Youth Hostel window, I could see small sparkling fairy lights of villages, reflecting on the water.

We walked down to town and had a meal, but this time we were not allowed to go into the kitchen to choose. Delphi was pleasant, and such a clean place after Thessalonica, but everything was expensive and aimed at attracting the tourist. One shop, we went into, had a lovely white suit on a model, and as I looked at it, to my horror, I saw a moth about two and a half inches long, with a wingspan of four inches. I had never seen anything so big and monstrous in my life before, and I rushed out of the shop in terror. The saleswoman laughed and knocked it down, and said that her daughter, too, was scared of moths, but when she went to pick it up the wretched thing was still alive.

Day 11   4th October

DELPHI. TO ATHENS GREECE

Today we sat by a river for lunch. One man on the coach has got an upset stomach. I'm glad I wasn't the first. It happens to everyone on these overland journeys.

This morning, rising long before light, at 5.15 a.m., a few of us left the youth hostel in Delphi to climb up the mountain behind the village, to watch the sunrise over the Apollo's Stadium. When we left it was still dark, and the moon was shining brightly. We walked along the road, behind the village.

It wound its way up past cottages, where people were busy harnessing donkeys with baskets and bundles, ready to make an early start for work. As the donkeys strode along, the bells around their necks jangled daintily, in time with their clopping feet on the cobbled pathways. The bells echoed through the village, increasing, as many more donkeys started off. The air was fresh and cool, and there was a stillness about the village, except for us, and the donkeys.

Soon we came to a very steep pathway, and we climbed up to the top of the mountain. I kept sliding out of my wooden sandals because they wouldn't bend with my feet, and my toes couldn't grip them. Air got thinner, and cooler, although we grew hotter, and we stopped now and again to rest, gasping for air. I could hear my heart thumping in my ears, and my lungs felt as if they would burst through overstrain, or collapse through lack of air. I couldn't tell which. In fact, if I hadn't got up, dressed, and fought my way up to the top of the mountain before I was properly awake, I'm sure I wouldn't have made it!!

Once at the top, it was worth every ounce of effort, for there below us was the Apollo Stadium and Temple, gradually lighting up as the sun rose higher. It was a peaceful, wonderful sight, as its rays spread out across the valley, to the opposite side of the mountain, to the Apollos, and over to the bay on our other side. The sea looked misty blue, and the surrounding mountains were warm and pink, as the early morning mist rose from the valleys.

After sitting watching, for an hour or so, we climbed down into the valley and walked around the stadium and temple before any tourists arrived. The sun, by now, was shining through the pine trees onto the ancient pillars beyond. That sight was unforgettable.

After visiting these, we walked along the road until we came to a famous old spring, in which we dipped our feet to cool off. As we walked further along this lovely road, with a mountain on one side and valley on the other, we admired the different types of trees, and bushes bearing bright orange berries. The sight was magnificent.

Our hearts were cheered even more, when we unexpectedly came across a little café overlooking the valley, with tables and chairs outside on a veranda. We certainly couldn't miss this opportunity of rest, and treating ourselves to a bit of comfort, so we sat down for a while and drank some Turkish coffee. This was the first time I had ever tasted that drink, and I fell in love with it at once. I was told that the sugar had been cooked with the coffee. It was strong and sweet and served in a small cup, with a tumbler of cold water to drink alternately.

Relaxing and basking in the sun's warmth, we looked down into the tree-covered valley where an occasional streak of smoke, slowly, rose from a bonfire. We saw the sea beyond. It was wonderful. I felt so grateful, to be there on holiday enjoying it all, while other people were working hard. At that moment I was leading a lady's life.

Then we walked on to see another temple, and from here we wended our way back. Passing the museum with its well-preserved mosaics, and also passing some of our party, who had only just got up and had missed the splendour of the day.

We arrived back at the hostel at about 9.30 a.m., by then it was extremely hot indeed, so we purchased some grapes and ate them on the balcony. We were later invited to see a couple of the boys' rooms in their fabulous hotel. They had a beautiful place, with stone floors downstairs and several fur rugs on the floors, but the view from their room was the same as from our hostel, and we got our accommodation for 3/9, and with a shower!!

The coach left Delphi at 1 p.m. and we had a short, mountainous drive to **Athens,** arriving there about 4.45 p.m. Eight of us set off to find the hostel, but after walking half an hour, we found that it had moved four days before. So we had to find another.

By then we had picked up a German boy, so he, and one of our boys, our only hostelling boy, went off to find where the hostel had moved to. On finding it was 15 km away, we decided to take the bus to the second youth hostel in Athens. Two hours later, we arrived.

What an old dump it was. To start with it had a large open-air courtyard, and as Athens had had torrential rain and floods that day, it was flooded. The girls' toilets were out of action, so it was all of us using the one, in the boys stinking old loo, which was a hole in the ground type, so when you pulled the chain, water rushed up the hole and drowned your feet, so because of that, and the smell, we decided it was better to stay dirty and not wash.

That evening nine of us went for a meal nearby. We first, had to go into the kitchens, to choose our food. Then sat outside at tables which were on a slope, so when the plates were set on the table, if you didn't watch out, your food slid off your plate onto the persons next to you.

The German boy sat at my table and he, thinking I was Australian said that he didn't like the British way of life. He thought it was boring the way they watched television and lazed around on Sundays. When he discovered I was British he was embarrassed, but I couldn't help agreeing with a lot of what he said, and it didn't worry me at all. I just found it amusing to hear what some foreigners thought about Britain.

We were on our way back to the hostel, very tired indeed after our long day out, when we passed a cake shop. We just couldn't resist them, so we each had a cake, which was served on a silver plate with a knife and fork, and a glass of water. It was a great luxury.

Once back at the hostel, it was a comfort to see a cat crouching guard outside our room, just waiting for any mice that might decide to come from between the crates of beer bottles, or from between the creaky floorboards. Our room was number 13 and was well apart from the others. It was surrounded by old brushes, buckets, bottles, and pans, as well as plenty of water over the floor. Our window led out into the street, which anyone could climb in and out of without much effort at all.

I found it interesting observing first-hand differences in the world. Climate, vegetation, scenery, and wildlife. Spoken languages and written scripts. Customs and costumes were unfamiliar. Moslem mosques and calls to prayer. Different head coverings and clothing are worn according to various religious beliefs. In some places, it was advisable not to wander about alone.

Day 12   5th October

ATHENS

Today was our free day in **Athens**. So after a hasty breakfast, I sped back to the hotel to pick up a couple of the others.

Travelling alone on Athens buses was an experience. The buses were frequent, but got crammed to capacity. I soon discovered that it wasn't a case of first in the queue, first on, but whoever was the best fighter, and pushed the most. I noticed that the centre of the queue usually got on first, so moved along to where the door would be on the second bus. Then when that bus came, I quickly jumped on.

I had a second breakfast with my friends, at the hotel, and then we went to the Acropolis to meet some of the others. We walked in single file along steep, narrow passages that ran, between small, whitewashed cottages. There were lots of steps. Old people were sitting in the sunshine enjoying the silence and peace. After tripping over dozens of cats, we eventually reached the Acropolis and met the others.

The Acropolis was much larger than I expected, being comprised of several old ruins. The most well-known is the Parthenon. It was lovely to walk around those old ruins and look down on the city beneath. I was under the impression that Athens consisted only of ruins and discovered that this was just a minute old romantic section, that I had heard about, so was disappointed to find that most of it was a dirty old city like other cities, and the noise of traffic almost deafening.

Later we ambled our way down, over the cobbles, past men selling postcards, pictures, maps, and other souvenirs until we came to the old market. Here cobblers, and scrap metal stalls, were plentiful. We looked around for a while in the heat, then decided to go to the Bank.

It took one hour, of standing in a queue, to change money. An embarrassing moment came when I suddenly remembered that the traveller's cheque, I wanted to change was still in my money belt, which was under my dress. So I discretely poked about through the gaps at the waist, hoisted up my petticoat, undid the zip pocket on the belt, and took out the cheque. I felt pleased to be so successful. Then, suddenly I stepped back, over a ventilator in the floor, and a draught of wind blew my skirt up over my head. That was so embarrassing, and people laughed.

After the bank, we sat in the square in the sun and drank Turkish coffee, as the shops had shut from 1 p.m. to 4 p.m. We wandered about for the afternoon and ate lumps of meat on a long stick, with a chunk of bread. They were called shish kebabs. This tasted good and would be OK for parties. I had never seen these before.

Later we walked through a park that had tropical plants, a bird sanctuary, and a small zoo. Out in the street again, we bartered with stallholders, I found this fun but didn't buy anything in the end. Then we had a meal in a garden, we had meat and macaroni with chips.

I left the others at a cake shop and went back to the centre of Athens to buy Malaria tablets, but the chemist shop hadn't got any. It took me a quarter of an hour to find the street, where I could get the bus back again.

I found the others by the Temple of Zeus and after a cake, with water, we went up to the Acropolis and sat on the grass watching Son et Lumiere, or Sound and Light, which was fashionable in that era, and told the history of a building, adding lighting effects and music.

As a voice boomed out, "The hill where we all do gather, you are on the very spot where Athenians of old would flock to hear the most beautiful tongue on this earth spoken to the greatest people of the world. The Golden days of Athens."

We chuckled as we thought of ourselves there now, instead, sitting in the cheapest seats at the back on the grass, and Dorothy even managed to disgrace us all by producing some wet washing from her bag and placing it on the fence to flutter dry in the breeze. How times had changed!

The voice went on," The city of Theseus, founder of Athens. Athens my slumbering goddess crouched in the shadow of the sacred rock. Oh, Athens a grain of stone out of a barren place, now born from the silver sea, a land of marble, adorned with beauty."

So the history of Athens unfolded. Lights flickered and changed showing up the Acropolis in all its grandeur. We heard of heroes who had marched on.

"Whoever then who has a heart, a soul, a mind thou could hardly refrain from speaking of others without exaggerating," said Aeschylus.

"How could one exaggerate?" said a listener,

"Is not Athens perfect?"

The lighting was fascinating as it changed, to give atmosphere, and blended most beautifully with the music. Brightly the Acropolis shone as Hercules said,

"This land upon which the same race has always worked was bequeathed to us free by our ancestors, because of their work. Our forefathers deserve our praise, yet even more so our fathers. For to this heritage, they have added the power we now withhold. Return the past decades. I speak to thee, elder citizens of this land, do we remember?"

The lights faded away as the elder citizens said over and over again,

"We do remember O Hercules."

In the darkness, creepy music sounded forth as the voices of the past talked one with another in fear.
Suddenly the scene changed, and voices were heard to say,

"The ruthless king's anger hovers over us. Darius has assembled his forces against all who wish to live in freedom. The cities of our Athenic land have been burned to ashes. The tyrant has become the leader and is now leading the enemy to our shore. The mercenaries of Xerxes, the Persians, have crowded the sandy beaches."

Lights flashed red and yellow, giving a very realistic effect of burning when the Athenians attacked.
Lights darted about as the barbarians pursued the Athenian men. Anguish befell the city. Athenian voices lamented,

"Alas, we suffer O God. The daughters of Athens cringe beneath Barbarian rule."

Cold shivers ran down my spine as I heard these blood-curdling cries. Flaming lights licked the Acropolis. News quickly came. Darius was dead and Xerxes was higher than unbounded ambition. Like marching swarms of battling ants, the troops of Xerxes assembled in Cappadocia, had crossed Frigia. Confusion struck. What were they to do?

"The gods will help you if you help yourselves. See all, and fear nought," was the advice.

The lights of Athens looked like fairyland as we sat on the hill, and the noise of traffic and the busy city rose up to meet us, as we listened to the history.

"We will leave our city and fight on the sea."

It seemed hard to imagine all this happening as I looked at Athens now.

The washing was drying on the fence by the time the Athenians set off to fight the Persians.!!
Persians hurled arrows of burning tar, over the barriers built by Athenians, who refused to leave the city. It was a bloodthirsty battle. They ransacked the sanctuary and set fire to the Acropolis. Some men ran away, and others sank into prayer within the Temple walls.

Red lights flashed off and on, giving a superb effect of flames licking the Acropolis. From the hill woefully they watched the raging blaze devour the city. The Athenians returned for combat.

War raged at sea. The ships crammed their brazen powers against each other. The sea sank away beneath a load of dirty wrecks and mute cold corpses.

"We are torn to shreds like fish caught in nets and crushed to a pulp by beating oars. Let us be free. What will become of us?" cried the Athenians.

"Quick to our ships."

"The people of Asia shall bow no more before this cruel Persian law. The ruthless king doth sob his ebbing power. The rule of force hath come to dust. This land with bloodshed stained. This isle of Ajax, which waves do whip, hath smothered, crushed, and crumbled the Golden day of Persians night."

We were thankful the war was over and breathed a sigh of relief as we heard Pericles say,

"Our fathers are worthy of praise, but it is to us, the living, who have now reached maturity, that the public owes its self-sufficiency in all things, in peace, as in war. What manner of might has led us to this power? The constitution which governs us has been given the name of democracy. Her purpose is the service of the greatest number. We are all equal before the law. Only personal merits open the way to honour. In our public life we are free and in no way do we spy on the particular behaviour of our citizens. We have given to the mind, countless refreshment. The greatness of our city draws to her treasures from the whole world. Athens is the school of Greece."

With these reassuring words from Pericles about our freedom, and confident that we were not spied upon, we took the, now dried, washing from the fence and went back to where we were staying. Happy that Athens had been rebuilt with magnificent monuments, superb in their greatness and congruent in their beauty and grace.

The light effect, on the Acropolis, changing colours, whilst the history of Athens was being told was beautiful, and remains in my mind. On the way back we bought pancakes wrapped around warm cooked meat, tomato, and shredded cabbage in oniony mayonnaise.

Day 13   6th October

ATHENS TO THESSALONICA

This morning we left the hostel and got a bus to meet the others. The bus came up crowded and all our queue pushed their way on, except me, so I waited for the next bus. Fortunately, I had put my bus fare in my pocket, because one of the girls had, unbeknown to me, taken my purse as a practical joke, and when she found that I had not got on her bus, she was panic-stricken and tried to get off, but couldn't do so, until they were nearly at their destination, where she got off and tried to find me on the next bus. Eventually, she turned up, and between us, we had kept the coach waiting half an hour, and were not too popular. I was given three letters from home on the bus and that made me very happy.

Morning coffee break was taken at a place down by the seaside, and I paddled in the sea, which was so warm. There was a most picturesque scene, by the sea. In a field, a black horse was grazing, with beautiful mountains behind. I could imagine it framed, as a painting, on the wall.

The remainder of the journey covered ground we had already been over and took us back to Thessalonica. Lunch break was taken at Pharsalus, a hot, dirty town full of restaurants and flies. In 48 BC, near here, the famous Battle of Pharsalus was fought, between Julius Caesar and Pompey the Great. Back in Thessalonica, we stayed in the Youth Hostel, where we previously stayed.

People ask me what it was like to travel all that way, on a bus, with so many people. Here is a glimpse.

There was quite a variety of people on the bus. I was one of the youngest. There were only ten British, the others were New Zealand and Australian. Most of the crowd was not so bad, but some people got a bit waring, by now. The thought of having to put up with six more weeks of them nearly drove me crazy.

The older ones were the trouble. Some of them kept shutting windows, without asking, and the younger ones, kept opening them again, and this caused bad feelings. They criticized the younger ones, worried about space, and getting on and off the bus, in fact about most things.

Some of them thought, that because they had known each other for about ten days, they had the right to pass opinions, or be nosey. The young crowd was alright, far more adaptable. The youngsters were not set in their ways and wanted to be friendly and enjoy life.

This was an example of community life in a confined space, for too long, and, at times, I didn't think much of it. People managed the cramped, tiring situation in diverse ways.

For me, there is nothing like freedom and being able to shake people off occasionally and have breathing space. There was one boy who hardly spoke to anyone, and I think he was wise

I will always remember the wise philosophy, of Gill Pardoe, who sat next to me. It sounded selfish at first but proved to be correct in the end. There were one or two people who got through the journey only because other people waited on them, and when they said to her,

"Will you carry one of my bags for me, or hold this?" she would reply,

"No, certainly not, if you can't manage your luggage, you should not have brought so much."

Then when people began to get fractious with each other on the bus she would say to me,

"Quick, Elizabeth, put your sunglasses on and shut them all out."
We would both dive for our glasses, put them on, and sat there laughing. It certainly worked for us.

Day 14   7th October

THESSALONICA TO ALEXANDROUPOLIS

Some of us caught a bus from the Youth Hostel, to catch the coach, and the bus broke down, so we had to catch another. The coach left at 8 a.m. and we drove straight to Kavalla. On the way be passed by Philippi and saw the old Roman road leading from Kavalla to Philippi.

Kavalla is a fishing town nestling below the mountains, and we stopped here for approximately one and a half hours to swim at the place where St Paul first set foot in Europe. It was gorgeous, swimming in the warm, clear, turquoise sea, then basking on the sand in the sunshine. We had to pay to go on the beach, but it was worth it, for there were showers and changing rooms. The beach looked as if it had been put there, because everywhere else was rocky. After a glorious time on the beach, we went back to the coach and had not gone far down the road, when we got a puncture. So whilst Frank, the driver, was changing the wheel, some of us walked into Kavalla itself and saw women and men sitting on the quay industriously mending nets. The remainder of the party had stayed in the town. We went swimming and then bought delicious shish kebabs, from a man in the street who had a stove, come shop, on wheels.

The drive to **Alexandropoulos** was fairly short. When we got there, about a third of the party slept out under the pine trees for the night, it was great. Before bed, a crowd of us wandered up into the town to dine, and all the population were out promenading along the street and all across the road, so no traffic could come through. It was a bit like carnival day. Back at the campsite Stephanie and John, a New Zealand couple of the party let us use their chalet to wash and change. The wife turned out to be Baptist and the husband was Presbyterian. They were a lovely quiet couple, who had married in England and were on their way home. They kept themselves to themselves quite a lot.

WEEK THREE

Day 15 8th October

ALEXANDROUPOLIS TO ISTANBUL

Today we are crossing into **Turkey**. After rolling up sleeping bags, packing up camp beds, and a quick glimpse at the sea, we were off on the bus for Turkey. A break of half an hour was taken at Alexandropoulos in order to spend the last odd coins of Greece. I bought an Alexandrite stone that I might have put into a ring. We had a laugh at one of the kiosk owners. When I tried to buy a stamp, he went crazy, trying to tell me that he hadn't got a stamp for such a small sum, then dismissed us in disgust. We tormented him by coming back for chewing gum. I think he was glad to see the back of us.

Postcard sent home **8 October Greece/Turkey**
"Greece was a beautiful country, and I liked the food."

Soon we arrived at the **Greek frontier**, where a break of about ten to fifteen minutes was taken in order to deal with formalities. Next was the **Turkish border**, with a similar break for the same reason. On reaching Turkey we were once more advised against going out alone, or unescorted in Middle East countries. We had first been told not to do so in Yugoslavia, because the people from there, onwards, have a habit of promenading in the evenings and they are out, idly, looking at people.

The journey took us on to Istanbul. We stopped on the way for lunch on the outskirts of a town by the sea, where men with guns were patrolling, which was alarming, to say the least. This was our first encounter with seeing such people. The route was very pretty, winding back and forth by the sea, weaving away, and losing sight of it, then seeing it again.

We were told that at one time, a man named Ataturk, ruled Turkey, and amongst the many things he did were, abolition of women's veils, introducing caps to prevent men from bowing to Allah, and touching heads on the ground. He turned a mosque into a museum, abolished Arabic lettering, and modernized Turkey to western standards. All these things were done against public opinion. He was an outstanding man and worked a great deal without sleep, taking drinks to keep him going. He got a lot done.

On reaching **Istanbul**, the first thing we saw was the breached 15th-century wall. At one time Constantinople was the capital of the East Roman Empire, and it was inhabited by Greeks. In 1453 the Turks stormed the city and breached the wall with gunpowder. This is thought to be the first-time gunpowder had been used in Europe.

The Turks lifted boats overland, through the wall, and to the Golden horn. This was a great victory. It is only their religion that makes Greeks in Greece different from Greeks in Turkey, but they still dislike each other.

The party split into two in Istanbul. The wealthy, older ones stayed in a hotel in the new posh part of the town, whilst the remainder of us stayed in the Duro Pallas Hotel in the old part. Actually, although it was in a rough area, it was very conveniently situated. The boats of the Bosphorus were a stone's throw away, and the markets and mosques were within walking distance.

Several of us went out for dinner to a restaurant that was recommended by the courier. It was clean and tidy, and the waiter was extremely helpful and obliging. We asked him to recommend a Turkish dish and he told us of a meat dish, which, he said, was a meal in itself, which required no vegetables with it. Well, when it came, we were shocked. It only consisted of two tablespoons of meat and gravy and wouldn't have kept a flea alive. We wondered if the Turks were light eaters, or if we were greedy. Mind you, the meat was very tasty. Anyway, we then ordered rice with it, and John, the waiter, said we could fill up on anything we liked, free of charge, so we had cake, tea, and a bottle of water.

About 9.30 p., fifteen to twenty of us went, by taxi, to the Karavan nightclub. The taxi tore along recklessly weaving in and out of traffic and up a steep, narrow road. That was an adventure in itself. When it suddenly shot off in the wrong direction, Frank, who was with us, made the taxi driver stop and we got out and walked.

What a walk! There were loads of men promenading, and what an odd lot they were as well! Some of them walked along with their arms around each other, and the others kept pinching and touching us girls. It was really unnerving and creepy. Even our escorts didn't have any effect, these chaps still took the liberty of pinching. I think they had a cheek.

We found that the floor show didn't start until 11 p.m., so we had another walk around. Then after buying a drink of orange we returned to the nightclub.

I was jolly glad of that orange drink because it had quenched my thirst and was bought for me. Whereas a drink of lemon in the club cost 11 lire, but there was no entrance fee.

The club was in a small room underground, and looked quite cosy, with soft lights and music, but the music wasn't very soft, in fact, it was jolly noisy, and I was sitting next to it.

A waiter put salted peanuts on our table and asked for 2.50 lire for them. We thought this an imposition and refused to have them, whereupon he said that every table had to have them and that we must pay 2.50 lire. Vanessa got furious and announced in a loud voice, which still couldn't be heard above the band, that we didn't like peanuts, didn't want peanuts and were not going to pay for peanuts! The waiter then took the hint and said, "Very well madam" and took them away.

I only went to the nightclub for the experience and to see belly dancers of the East, at the cheapest place on our route. There was far more variety than I expected and was more like a cabaret. After a few general dancers, in came a group of four men, one played a fiddle and the other three did Russian-type dancing. There was also an eastern band, an acrobat group, and fire throwing.

There was, however, a young girl of about twelve in the group, who stood smiling and flashing her eyes at the men. I thought she was too young for that environment. Another group was candle dancers, they danced around and had to try to keep the candles alight. In between these acts were dancing girls. These I thought were crude, these girls were only young, and therefore not experienced in stripping and dancing gracefully. Instead of dancing smoothly and removing the veils without the audience noticing, they stopped to unhook clothing or got men to do this, which made the acts very crude indeed.

One girl chose one of our men, the shyest one, and asked him to dance with her. The poor fellow thought that he only had to dance, but soon discovered that he had to assist in her act   He was so embarrassed and wouldn't respond at all well, until she got angry, and the audience slow hand clapped him. We left at about 1 a.m. and went back to the hotel. It was an experience, and I did get to see belly dancers.

Day 16   9th October

ISTANBUL

I had such a leisurely day. It was really good. Breakfast was taken late at about 9.30 a.m. and we went out at about 10.30 a.m. Walking through the cobbled, dusty streets, where trolleybuses and cars hooted and barged their way about, we climbed the steep road to the Blue Mosque with its six minarets. This mosque was beautiful. It is the only mosque to have so many minarets.

Approaching the mosque from the courtyard, the first thing I noticed was the unusual door. It was rolled up leather, which had been engraved and painted, so everyone had to bow down as they entered. All shoes had to be removed before setting foot on the doorstep, covered with rush matting. When prayer time arrived, the leather door was rolled higher up, and a heavy string network hung in the space, which had to be lifted back by each entrant.

After hearing the people being called to prayer, we went inside at the invitation of a mosque official and watched the service. The priest stood by his mat leading the people in prayer, but at a certain point in the prayers, everybody crowded forward onto the platform with the priest. They were all packed closely together beside him, and the picture of Mecca. Every year Mohammedans have to offer a male lamb for each unmarried son in the family. If he is poor and can't afford a lamb, he may offer a chicken or a pigeon, but each animal must be a male.

Around the floor were long wooden boxes for shoes to be put, that had not been left outside, and even in the section divided off for tourists, these boxes had to be used. The tourists also had to sit on their feet to keep their legs covered. Inside was a most impressive sight and one which I shall always remember. There were many good quality red coloured carpets, all over the large mosque floor. Low-hung lights were suspended from wrought ironwork.

There were the beautiful blue walls and ceiling, which were hand-painted, to look like a mosaic.
They were a tremendous piece of craftsmanship, which must have taken ages to complete, and blended in beautifully with the leaded windows that were at the east end of the mosque, hence its name, Blue Mosque. All the other windows were plain glass.

The east of the mosque faces Mecca in Saudi Arabia, so this is the direction the people face in Turkey, but in Japan they face Southwest.

The mosque was supported by four huge pillars. By the Northeast pillar stood the preacher's chair, where he ascends the steps and sits crossed-legged on a cushion fairly high up, and addresses the congregation, on Fridays.

In the centre of the east wall is the priest's prayer mat, where he leads the people in prayer, and just near this is a picture of Mecca. To the right of this mat, very high up, and approached by stairs, is the pulpit, which is only used on Fridays, their religious day.

By the southeast pillar stood a small stone building where the assistant priest calls the people to prayer and where he prays. By the two west pillars stood two grandfather clocks, which chimed the hours.

On the four sides of the mosque were cloisters and balconies where the women worshippers knelt. I was told by a Muslim in the mosque that only men could pray in the floor space, because if women were there, they would distract them, from their prayers, and the men would be thinking of the women instead of God.

Many mosques, nowadays, have a microphone, on top of the minarets to save the assistant priest going up it five times a day. Prayers are said at sunrise, midday, mid-afternoon, sunset, and one hour after sunset.

Muhammadans have a rosary comprised of 33 beads, each representing the 33 years of Christ's life, and so they thank God 33 times. First of all, when they pray, they stand up with their hands behind their ears, signifying that they have cut out the world, and are only thinking of God. Then they bow forward, stand straight again, bend their knees, and kneel, then bow forward, touching their heads on the ground in front of them.

After leaving the mosque, where I recorded part of the service, we headed back towards the boats for a trip up the Bosphorus to the Black Sea. It was a beautiful, hot, sunny day and we bought our tickets, and then discovered that we had half an hour to spare, so as we had not had any lunch, we bought some mackerel in bread, with raw onion, from a vendor with a portable barbecue. The fish was so fresh and tasty, it was caught and cooked at once.

The boat called at every port on the route, and people crowded on. When we were in sight of the Black Sea the boat stopped on the Asia side of the Bosphorus and we got out. The village was a quaint fishing place, with its wooden houses, dusty, unmade roads, and little fishing boats.

We tried to walk to the Black Sea, but every exit from the village was forbidden territory, as it was a military zone, so we had to stay in the village. After looking around, we went into a cafe for refreshment and sat watching the sun sink low behind the mountains.

Soon our boat arrived, and we boarded. As we set off, I could see tiny fishing boats setting out to sea, with their bright oil lamps beaming from the backs. Our boat had a searchlight that constantly scanned the water looking for objects and boats, and the corks on fishing nets shone up luminous in the beam and looked intriguing and attractive.

After a while on the boat it got cool, so Gill and I went inside to join the others and got talking to an elderly Turkish couple. The husband was a physician and really reserved, whilst his wife kept chatting away to us and told us a couple of times that this was her second husband, but that he wasn't such a bad old fellow! Poor chap, no wonder he was shy!! She also took delight in telling us what a brilliant family she came from, of how her father and brothers were physicians, of how musical she was, and what clever children she had. She was quite entertaining.

Once back at the hotel, the four boys and two or three of the girls came into our room and we sat talking and discussing characters, and reading characters, until about 1 a.m. in the morning. It was great fun.

Day 17   10th October

ISTANBUL

This morning we visited the Top Kapi Sarayi or
Topkapi Palace Museum. It was here that the Sultans
lived and kept their Harems. The gardens were pretty
in the sunlight, against the palace walls.

One room contained chine from Persia, China,
Japan, France, and Turkey which dated from about the
15th century. Other rooms contained Sultans' garments.
Two of the men had died wearing their gowns and had
to have them cut off, one was bearing bloodstains from
300 years ago.

Other rooms exhibited beautiful jewels set in
swords, thrones, crowns, and cradles, whilst others
contained miniatures, paintings, and seals. I saw
something that I thought was extremely good and that
was the Koran written in miniature books, and also
parts of the Koran inscribed on rice seeds.

Officials were obliging and pleased to show us
around their rooms. After our visit, we sat out on a
veranda overlooking the Bosphorus and the mosques of
Istanbul.

As we sat admiring the view and the hustle and
bustle of ships moving back and forth, an English chap
came and joined us and stayed with us for the rest of
the day. He was a salesman in communist countries for
ICI, and his name was Mike. He was a typical
Englishman, with his polite, precise manners. He came
in useful because he could speak several languages and
acted as an interpreter for me in a chemist shop, where
he spoke Serb Croatian.

After walking around the museum for about five
hours, we decided to have some lunch. The place where

we ate was scruffy, like most of the cafes. The meal consisted of a very plain pastry-like mixture, similar to Ravioli, with a trace of meat and cheese. We ended with a cup of tea.

Our next move was to catch an 86 bus to the Mosaic Museum. It came up crowded, but an old lady who was getting off deliberately made sure that I had her seat. The others thought I must have looked weak and helpless.

The Kariye Museum was impressive, with the various mosaics depicting Bible stories. I was impressed by one which represented the resurrection. God was descending from the clouds and as the graves opened, so He stretched out His hands and pulled the people out of the graves, up into Heaven. The mosaics were old Byzantine and some of the most beautiful of that time. The Turks converted it into a mosque and added a minaret. The mosaics have recently been uncovered and it has been turned into a museum. The mosaics belong to the 13th to 15th century

After this, we all caught a bus back to the Kapali Carsi Market. This is one of the most interesting places in Istanbul. Originally it was built by Fatih Sultan Mehmet the Conqueror, Ottoman sultan who ruled in the 15th century.

Bedesten is the style of these old Ottoman structures, where valuable objects were stored and sold. Every kind of article, especially antique carpets, jewellery, gold, silver, and other metal goods, were sold. Antiques of the Ottoman period were once sold by auction.

It is the most famous and interesting covered bazaar in the world and looks like a big city. It would have been quite easy for us to get lost, for sixty lanes led off in all directions, leading to around 4,000 shops selling interesting objects.   Local pop music blared out from loudspeakers all over the bazaar. This was wailing to a one-stringed instrument and sounded exactly like the priest calling from the mosque, except that he didn't have any music.   Whilst we were there, there was a power strike in part of the bazaar. so candles were lit and flickered in the shops. Then suddenly all the lights went on again, and as they did, a great cheer went up.

It was fun bargaining with the salesmen, who always set their prices far too high, knowing full well that the purchasers would barter them down. Martin was particularly good at bargaining, and it was funny to listen. He would state a price and the salesman would refuse, so Martin would make to go away. This then led the salesman to call him back and drop his price, which Martin still would not accept. This went on until at last a fair price was agreed. Martin bought some slippers for his mother, and the young salesman called him a capitalist at the end of it all. This made us all roar with laughter because that was just what we had nicknamed him, for staying in the best hotels! Just for the fun of it, the salesman let the next customer have slippers for one lira less.

After the market, we went for a meal and then said Goodbye" to our English friend and went back to the hotel.

Day 18   11th October

ISTANBUL TO ANKARA

Leaving behind the hustle and bustle of old Istanbul, we crossed the bridge over the Golden Horn to new Istanbul, to collect the rest of our party. Soon we were on the ferry and crossing the Bosphorus into **Asia.** The road went beside the **Marmara Sea**, which sparkled in the sun. The mist was rising, and beautiful clouds were beginning to cap mountains on the distant shore. These appeared pale blue, behind the veil of rising mist, and the sea was silver, as it shimmered in the sun.

Down by the shore, a woman walked, while her little child played on the sand. Her long gown blended beautifully into the surroundings under the leaning willow tree.

We crossed the mountain pass of Bolu and stopped at the top for lunch. The view down into the valley was picturesque, with the many deciduous trees that were red and gold. The afternoon drive led through very arid, flat, then rolling hill country. Quaint villages, with houses made of wood, and small bricks of mud clay, looked Tudor-styled. Many houses and mosques were made of wood, and I saw one wooden mosque, at midday, with the Imam standing in the minaret calling the people to prayer. Another small mosque had prayer mats hanging over the fence to air.

Women wore baggy trousers, loose coats, and veils. Children ran about in colourful clothing. We stopped to buy raffia pots and trays from young girls who were selling by the roadside. An older woman sat cross-legged making items for them to sell cheaply.

Soon we arrived in **Ankara,** which is now the capital of Turkey. It is a modern city nestling in the valley between two hills. Ankara appeared as a dirty, creepy place. There was no necessity to go out, so Dorothy, Sue, and I ate in our room and sat chatting.

Day 19   12th October

ANKARA TO URGUP

Leaving the Hotel Imperial at 8.30 a.m., we went to
visit the Mausoleum of Mustafa Kemal Ataturk
who was the first president of Turkey and served from
1923 until he died in November 1938.

It was set up on a hill overlooking Ankara. Millions
of lire were spent on erecting this awe-inspiring
monument, and much effort is made to keep it looking
respectable. At the top of a flight of wide stone steps,
stood a military man, guarding the impressive, long
stone pathway.

Three statues of Ataturk stand on the left-hand side
of the path, and these represent his supplying the needs
of the people. Three more statues stand on the right.
Between each flagstone, the grass is allowed to grow,
which, on looking back to the entrance, looks like a
green carpet

Fir trees line the pathway giving an enclosed
atmosphere, suggestive of homeliness. At the far end
of the long path is a quadrangle, surrounded by
buildings, which contain things appertaining to
Ataturk, such as his different cars.

At one end, at the top of a flight of stairs, is a large
Roman-style building. Inside is a large, empty room
with a highly polished floor. At the far end, lays the
tomb of Ataturk. Standing by the freshly laid wreaths,
in front of this great grey marble tomb, I could feel the
air of Turkey blowing in through the window, across
the tomb. I had the feeling that Turkey still loved this
great man, and was protecting his very remains, and
preserving his memory.

The road out of Ankara was dusty in places and ascended up over the plain, arid hills, which lay in an undulating mass, for miles. At times, they looked like patchwork quilts of varying shades of brown, against the blue sky above, with puffs of cotton wool clouds. Large flocks of sheep streamed down between the hillocks, whilst other small, multi-coloured flocks scratched amongst the stubble and scrubland.

The houses we passed seemed to be coated in mud and allowed to dry and crack. Occasionally a door stood open, and inside I could see a woman sitting cross-legged on the floor, wearing a long garment, and a white veil wound about her neck and head. Women did their washing in troughs by the well and hung the washing, to dry, on bushes, or from their windows.

For quite a while we had been looking for a suitable place for a "bush stop," but as the countryside was so sparsely vegetated, there were hardly any trees. Suddenly, we came to some, and the coach stopped opposite a mud house, with brass pots and pans out in the sun. No sooner had we stopped than all the ladies piled out and rushed to the trees and bushes across the road, opposite this house.

The woman at the house put down her water pot and came rushing across the road. She came at such a speed that her trousers fluttered and flapped in the breeze, and there she stood, arms akimbo, gazing in amazement at all these women using her garden as a toilet!!! Well, who was to know it was a garden? To us, it just looked like a clump of trees opposite a house. Then when the woman got on the bus again, and the men got out, she realised what was happening and laughed, and even let someone take her photo.

Continuing our journey, we passed Lake Tuz of Anatolia, which is a Salt Lake, and was very dried up and white around the edges. Besides this large lake, women and girls packed straw into sacks and tied them onto the backs of donkeys, which stood patiently waiting, blinking in the sunlight.

There were ridges of finely folded hills bearing numerous downward indentions as if streams had once flowed. Their rock was composed of various beautiful shades of colours, such as rust, maroon, green, brown, and yellow, and was most impressive. To the other side of us lay a large flat expanse of dry land that was once used for cultivation. I could imagine the people working hard in the fields at sowing and harvest time, but just now the fields were dormant. In places, dust rose from the ground, and in one place I actually saw a small whirlwind.

The lunch stop was taken at an isolated collection of stalls around a restaurant. It was like a wild west scene, and I expected to see cowboys come galloping up to tie up their horses, but instead of cowboys, a local bus pulled up for petrol. The bus looked as if it would fall apart, and it was packed to capacity with men and women who stared at us in amazement. I wonder what they thought of us. Perhaps they had never seen western women with bare arms before.

The petrol was pumped into the coach through the back window to a tank inside. Those fumes must have nearly suffocated the people. The buses had exhaust pipes like chimneys, they went up into the air and belched out exhausts from the top. As the bus went off down the road, clouds of dust followed behind it, and the packets, parcels, and sacks secured to the roof rack were almost obscured.

The drive on to **Urgup** was one of the most impressive, and beautiful sights I had ever seen. Urgup and the Gerome valley are the consequence of volcanic eruptions, and soil erosion, combined with the tilt of the land. All these factors have resulted in a most unusual land structure and colour formation. The landscape looks lunar and rather weird, Rocks are shaded colours of white, cream, yellow, pink, orange, reds, and mauves. According to the position of the sun, different colours predominate, at various times of the day.

As we drove away, through the surrounding mountains, bright sunshine adorned with abundant colours, and houses carved out of the rocks could be clearly seen. These houses are now mostly uninhabited, so Urgup was like a ghost town. On route, scenes like this could not be missed, so we had one or two photo stops.

After looking in at Urgup, we then went by coach, to the **Valley of Goreme**, set amid these coloured rocks, out of which churches and houses, were carved. Originally 300 were carved, but now only about six remain intact, due to vandalism.

We wandered in and out of churches and houses, observing frescoes painted on ceilings and walls, but noticed that all the eyes of people were scratched out. Houses possessed rock-hewn tables and chairs. These troglodyte dwellings were where the first Christians lived. It was quite a scramble climbing up and down rocky steps to visit these places.

On the way back from Goreme the sunset was beautiful, without a cloud in the sky. It was so colourful, and breath-taking, with the shape of the mountains silhouetted against it.

Whilst we were there a film company was setting up to make a film called, "The Three Green Dogs."
The film people stayed at our hotel, and, in the evening, the locals put on a party for us all, which cost 5/- each.

We watched Turkish dancing, then we got invited to join the dance too. At one time they elected me to be the leader and wave the white scarf as we danced. We listened to their music, and I managed to tape some.

Towards the end of the evening some of them tried to get too friendly, so Malcolm, Barry, Dawn, and I left, and we had coffee and a chat in Sandra's room. Frank the driver, came looking for me because they thought I had gone missing, which was very good of him.

Day 20   13th October

URGUP TO ANTIOCH

Last night camping was the coldest night I had spent in my life. It was bitterly cold. I lay awake all night but fell asleep about 5 a.m. and so missed the Imam calling from the mosque. I had been looking forward to that. We hastily packed up our beds and bags and walked down to the village for breakfast. Breakfast was the best on route so far, and was substantial, for as well as bread and honey, there was omelette and tea. It was certainly enough to keep us going for the day.

The morning was clear and bright, with a slight nip in the air. Sunshine on the surrounding mountains emphasized their colour and illuminated the houses carved out of rocks.

As we drove away through the mountains, everywhere shone in abundant colour. Later we came to one of the ancient camel caravans stopping places. All that is left of it now is an old gateway. Here natives came to speak to us, and we had quite an amusing time because nobody understood what anybody was talking about, but all pretended that they did.

On the way out of Urgup, we called at a vineyard. The smell was enough for me, and it didn't look particularly hygienic. We were taken around and shown where the wine was bottled, and where it was allowed to stand to allow scum to form. Then the part that made me laugh was, that after people had purchased wine, we went across the road to see the first stage of processing, and sure enough, there was a barefooted man treading grapes, as they were being shovelled out of a lorry. I do hope he'd washed his feet!

The journey to Antioch covered some of yesterday's ground, through low-lying arid land, and mountains. We could see the snow-capped **Taurus Mountains** in the distance, no wonder it was cold last night. Soon our roadway led up through, and over, these mountains, and the scenic quality was superb.

High rugged mountains, with grassy slopes, were a beautiful welcome sight, and an unexpected one, after the hot desert we had passed through. Now, we were more in the eastern sector of Turkey, which joins up with Iraq.

Lunch stop was taken by a mountain stream up in these lovely surroundings. There was a rock, out of which poured pure spring water. People were there, not only drinking it, but also taking off their shoes and socks and standing in it to wash their feet, hands, faces, and heads. A large notice was written in Turkish, but unfortunately, I couldn't read it, so I didn't know what was so special about this place, and nobody else seemed to either.

We travelled on through the Cilician Gates, the famous corridor through which many armies have passed, including Alexander the Great, Hadrian, and the Crusaders.

The day's drive was an exceptionally long one because we were scheduled to stop the night at Adana, but as this was not a very pleasant place it was arranged that we should go on to **Antioch.** Several of us got down together in the coach and had a good chin wag as it began to get dark, and then we had singsong until the older ones at the back complained that they were unnerved by the mountain pass and that our singing made them worse!!

This mountain pass had thirty-three hairpin bends and it was dark when we went over it. I had never before been over such a pass. One bend came directly after another, and the coach was so long that it kept scraping the slope of one bend as it went round the next.

Malcolm was singing softly as we went over this pass. He had such a pleasant, easy-to-listen-to voice that it was quite soothing. There were all these old dears behind us gasping and sighing away in absolute fear, and there was Malcolm singing folk songs and songs from musicals.

We arrived at Antioch at about 8 p.m. Some of us had to walk half a mile to the hotel. Once there, Gill, Annette and I found that we, each, had a linen cupboard to sleep in. A bed had been put in amongst the blankets and sheets. I got a reduction on these rooms and had them knocked down from sixteen and a half lire to 10 lire. There was one good thing about it, we had enough blankets in there to keep us warm forevermore, and it certainly made up for the night before when I simply froze.

There was chaos tonight at this hotel, everyone in our party, was complaining about something or other. They either didn't like their room, or hadn't got a room, didn't like the coach trip, or thought we had travelled too far in a day. Anyway, I think their trouble was that they were overtired and the last lap of the journey, over the mountains had just about finished them off. We had supper at about 9.30 p.m., I had stuffed vine leaves, and then I sat drinking tea in with Eva, Francis, and Valerie, and then to bed.

Day 21   14th October

ANTIOCH TO LATAKIA SYRIA

Close to Antioch is the Plain of Issus where the armies of Alexander and Darius fought in 333 BC. Antioch is the place where the Christians were first called Christians. It is said to be one of the three greatest cities of the world, only outranked by Rome and Alexandria. This morning was free and several of us went to visit a museum, containing archaeological finds. The weather was extremely hot as the sun beat down upon us.

We wandered through the marketplace, where people walked about carrying huge bundles on their backs, like beasts of burden, carrying tables, mattresses, colossal sacks, or planks of wood. Women walked sombrely in their black costumes, which swept the ground, and wearing yashmaks to cover their faces, partially or completely. Children played in the narrow alleyways, and sheep wandered casually about.

Antioch has a river running through her and is framed by a large mountain at the back, so she nestles between the two. We went to get Vanessa's sandal mended and one cobbler, not only got chairs out for all of us but also put paper down for her to stand on. The cost was only about one and a half pennies, old money. After walking about the cobbled marketplace for a while, we went back towards the hotel.

I ventured off on my own to the post office, but it caused such a stir amongst the people of Antioch to see a stray woman going around on her own, and almost nude in comparison to their women, who can hardly be seen behind their veils and gowns, that I was quite relieved to meet some of the others. We went into the men's gaming house for tea and that made up a peep show as well. Really, we didn't quite conform to the pattern of the eastern ladies.

We left Antioch, by coach, at 1 p.m. and drove to **Latakia**. On the way, we crossed from **Turkey into Syria**. Arab lettering and western lettering stood side by side on all signs and posters, and the numbering was also different from what we were used to, e.g. 0=5, and.=0, and 10=1.

It was dark as we went across the mountain passes to Latakia. When we arrived there, all the Capitalists were taken to a hotel, but the rest of us, who were the youngsters, were dropped in the town square and had to find our own accommodation in native hotels all amongst the Arabs. Gill, Vanessa, Sue, Dorothy, I, and the four boys stayed in one hotel. It was a trek up the stairs to the room, and men were trotting about in their pyjamas. It certainly was an odd, and unnerving, sight. We five girls shared one room to economize, and it worked out at about 4/- for bed. As our finances were good, we decided to go out for dinner, so we went to a restaurant down by the sea and sat eating for a couple of hours.

In Syria it is the custom to bring out lots of dishes of nuts, radishes, carrots, and cucumber, to nibble with a drink and dinner, so while we were waiting for our chicken and fish to cook, we sat chatting and eating nuts. Well, when the food arrived, we just couldn't believe our eyes, it was so good, in fact, it was worthy of photographs, which we had to take to prove that the peasants could feed sumptuously. After a wonderful meal, we went back to the hotel, and we all crammed into one room and had coffee and a chat.

WEEK FOUR

Day 22   15th October

LATAKIA TO BEIRUT LEBANON

This morning we left at 8 a.m. and didn't manage to get any breakfast because the service was too slow.

We went from **Syria into Lebanon**. In the Bible, Lebanon was referred to as a land flowing with milk and honey.

Lunch break was taken at **Byblos,** and we had quite a long while here, in fact, some people went swimming, but by the time we had found the beach, it was too late for a swim.

Byblos gave its name to the Bible and is an ancient place dating back to at least 7,200 BC. It was an ancient part of the Phoenicians and is the oldest continuously inhabited town in the world.

While we were there, excavation was taking place and three temples had been discovered. One 3000 BC, another 2200 BC, and one 1800 BC. In this last one, there is evidence that babies used to be sacrificed, also a freshwater well was found. People used to be buried in egg-shaped tombs to put them back into the posture of pre-birth. There are remains of seven walls, which were destroyed by earthquakes, two Phoenicians, one Amorite, one Egyptian, one Hyksos, one Assyrian, one Babylonian, and one Persian. Connected with this old castle are five crusades, British, French, German, Italian, and Spanish.

From Byblos, we drove along the most beautiful coast road to Beirut. The sea looked welcoming and blue under the sun's bright rays. On our journey, we passed olive groves, banana trees, orange trees, and of course grapevines. Some cotton plantations are still to be seen.

Beirut is a large seaport bounded at the back by hills and at night the lights twinkled and sparkled beautifully from the sea up to the mountains. Palm trees, bearing dates, grow in the city centre and down by the sea. They looked magnificent and erect.

The city is very noisy indeed. These eastern places are full of noise, but Beirut is more than the rest. Cars had loud engines, just as if the silencers had fallen off. Horns were constantly peeping and blowing most unnecessarily, every time one car passed another it blasted loud and long on the horn. People didn't talk quietly, they shouted, and waved their arms about.

Our hotel was in the city centre and had a fruit market at the back, and the main street in the front. So the noise was outrageous, with hooting, engines, voices, shuffling feet, and banging boxes, as well as loud arguments whilst bargaining. I began to wonder if I was getting old noticing this entire hubbub.

Beirut was hot and sticky. We wandered around a bit and then went for a snack. Some went to the pictures, but Dot, Sue, Vanessa, and I went back to the hotel for coffee. On the way we visited the market and were given raw, fresh dates to eat, they were good.

We also lost two more of our party at Beirut, for they had booked a passage on board a ship from there.

Day 23   16th October

BEIRUT

This morning about a dozen of us went to the English Church for the morning service. It was extremely hot outside, with only the buildings and date palms to give a bit of shade. The church was beautifully situated so that the doorway opened up onto a large balcony overlooking the sea.

Inside the church, it was quite plain, with pale blue walls, and not much ornamentation. There were a couple of large fans revolving which kept the building cool and comfortable. I thoroughly enjoyed the service, which was Harvest Festival. Fruit and flowers were decorating the church in a simple fashion. The service was followed by a communion service for all Christians and not just the Church of England, so I was able to participate. There are three other Baptists on this bus.

The minister mentioned in his sermon that, less than five hundred miles away from Beirut, which is within one hour's flying distance, people were dying of starvation. This thought was sobering and difficult for me to take in because in England I tended to think that starvation lay thousands of miles away, and beyond my reach, but to think that people are starving near at hand really shook me.

I still can't forget Skopje with its poverty and beggars and can still see the ragged children, in my mind, and hear the pathetic voices of parents and children begging for alms.   Begging is common in other eastern countries we have passed through, and poverty is even more predominant, but Skopje was my first sight of such things and therefore has made the deepest impression.

The minister said that to the starving people, Harvest Festival and the harvest hymns would appear a farce. I could well believe this too, for there we sat in our plenty, lacking nothing and surrounded by food, just in the lap of luxury, not only having all our needs met but all our wants as well. Then, there, on the other end of the scale were the people who did not even have their needs supplied, let alone their wants. There is surely something wrong with mankind, that they don't share and distribute around the world. I even feel that I've got more than I need in my case, and that's not much.

In the afternoon, five of us girls decided to go for a swim and were told the name of a pleasant beach which was Trabzon, not far out of Beirut. We set off for the bus and asked a policeman which bus to catch, whereupon he waved his arms, blew his whistle, and stopped a bus in the middle of the high street for us to get on. We paid our fare and after a long ride discovered that he had misunderstood the name and we were heading for Tripoli, which was miles away. The Arab name for Tripoli was Trablos, similar in sound to our beach Trabzon.

Anyway, the bus still jogged along, and the driver was shouting and gesticulating, all the time, whilst a boy at the back door kept shouting out the destination of the bus, which was Trablos so that anyone in the street would know where it was going and could stop the bus and hop on. People piled in with parcels and goods, and the bus kept stopping and starting, and the noise got worse and worse, shouting, and talking and hooters going in competition to the radio. When we realised that we were heading for the wrong place, we decided to alight at Byblos and visit the castle.

We went for a swim and got chatting with some local students, who invited us for a ride in their speed boat. The hills of Lebanon looked beautiful from the sea. It was marvellous speeding out to sea and watching the land get more distant, and then drawing up close to some coves again so that we could view the excavations. Once off the boat, these boys said that we could change in their cave. This was just like a little house, with electricity installed and glass windows in the ceiling, and one wall. Inside it was equipped with a divan and chairs, shower, toilet, and washbasin.

We said we would like to go up and see the castle. The guide who was showing people over the castle said he was sorry that the castle was shut but if we wanted to know anything he would willingly tell us because we were with his friends. He was in his late forties I should think. He told us the history of the castle, the remains they'd found and the period they were from.

After this, we all walked back down from the castle, and he offered to give us a lift to the bus stop. Once all five of us got inside the car, He said,

"Would you like to come for a cup of tea?"
So we said that we would like to, because he was interesting to talk to.

So he stopped outside a restaurant, that used to be an old crusader cave, which was now converted into a museum. Outside were historic remains of things that had been found in Byblos in excavations, such as old ploughs.

Inside there were ancient finds displayed in various places which gave the cave an old mystic atmosphere. There were grottos where chairs and tables were set. Some had stone seats. Shells containing little lights were displayed in alcoves.

In the small shop, was a glass cabinet full of jewellery, with precious stones. Out in these countries, you can buy exceptionally good stones, very cheaply, but you have to be clever to tell the difference between fake and genuine. Here they did sell really good stones. After looking around we sat down.

Through an archway, I sat watching the tall marram grass swaying gently in the breeze, silhouetted against the changing colours in the sky. The red glow was a beautiful sight as the sun was slipping behind the sea, and its large red ball slithered away

He asked us what we would like to drink. I just love their tea, which is black and sweet, so I had tea. Everyone else had a mineral drink. They laughed at me and said,

"Trust the English to have tea."

In Lebanon, they serve little dishes of nuts, carrots or cucumbers, and other things, with drinks. You never get just drinks.

We were busy talking away, men were drinking alcohol, and then they'd go and a few more came and went and returned with a few more men. It was not long before more and more men joined the party, and we were outnumbered.

One man was talking to Vanessa, and she was looking at some rings. The rest of us did not know what was happening, but he asked her if she would like one, and she said yes that she would. So he gave her a ring with a great big yellow stone and said that she could have it. She accepted the gift. The sun faded and died, and darkness was all about.

Then all these men suddenly asked us if we would like to go out with them for the evening and have dinner. We said that we were sorry, but could not, as we had to be back by half-past seven. They said,

"Oh, you can't go back tonight you've missed the bus." So we said,

"Well, we will walk."

"Oh no. You stay the night here." We thought,

" Hello, hello!" and said that we were sorry, but we could not do that. So we invented a chaperone. One of the girls said,

"No I'm afraid we have to report into a chaperone at half-past seven, and if we don't report, a search party will be sent out. So we have to go and report in." The men said,

"Oh, alright. We'll take you and you can report in and come out again." We said,

"We are not allowed out unless there are three of us."
So three said they would go but had no intention to at all.

At this point, the whole cave was plunged into utter darkness. Oh! My goodness! Were we scared!! I did not know what was going to happen next. I could not see a thing, because this cave was mostly underground, and it was pitch black. I grabbed hold of my camera and my bag, for a start.

I got up and said to Dorothy, who was next to me,

"Come on quick, let's go. Pass the word along."
So we all got up, and these men said,

"OK, alright," and lit a match, and we began to see our way out.

As we went out, all the lights came back on. So why they went off, whether accidentally, or on purpose, or not, I don't know, but all I can say is that I was absolutely scared. Particularly when they had tried to persuade us to stay the night.

They decided to give us a lift home. Once outside we piled into a car and then they talked together in Arabic, making plans. They then changed drivers and we were off. The young fellow was quite pleasant and drove us up the road, but when he turned off into a country lane, we demanded to know where he was going but he would not answer. We saw buses on the main road, so we said we would get out and get the bus, but he wouldn't hear of it. He turned his car around and stopped outside a house.

Another man came out in his car and followed us down the road. What was happening we did not know. He stopped, turned around, and we were instructed to get into that, as it belonged to one of their men, and he would take us back, as the others had business to attend to. This fellow looked honest, whereas the others, who we were already with, looked like rogues.

On the way back he got stopped by the police for having the car overloaded, but as his uncle was a policeman in the village, he was let off and didn't have to pay the fine. Anyway, we got back to Beirut, and he said,

"Tell us what hotel you'll be at, and I'll drop you there and wait for you."

We thought, "Oh no. No."

We thought he was just going to drop us. So we saw a hotel and I said,

"Stop here, this will do, this is near our hotel."

It was just around the corner and a couple of streets away. We thought he can't see us go in here, so I struck on an idea and said,

"You go up the road and park, and that will do fine, and come back and get us."

He believed us, fortunately, and went up the road, and round the corner to park. Meanwhile, we shot across the road, ran around the turnings, up the hill to our hotel, and got back in.

I was sharing a room with four people older than me, and we asked them if they would go out and buy us some supper.

We all came into my room and the people came back with food. We were telling them the exciting story and had just finished our supper when there was a knock at the door.

Margaret opened it and was expecting to see one of the other members of our party. To our dismay, there was this fellow who brought us in his car. He saw us and said,

"Is Miss Susanne there please?"

Well of course he'd seen her, so we couldn't say that no she wasn't. So Margaret said, "What do you want?"

He replied,

"I want the girls to come out."

"No. Sorry, they can't," she replied,

"Are you the chaperone?" he asked.

"Yes, the girls can't come out."

"Oh no, they must come."

"I must shut the door," she answered, and off he went,

When he'd gone, the girls went back to their room. Then a bit later he came again, and she told him we were not there. He couldn't make that out.

How he found the right hotel I just do not know. We were astonished for he not only found the right hotel but the right room too.

Malcolm, one of our boys came up and asked me if I would wash his hair. He seemed to be incapable of doing it himself and we girls took it in turns to do it, and it was my turn. He said he would escort me back afterwards to make sure I got back safely. It was a rambling hotel with dark corridors, and corridors going off corridors. To go to the toilets, we used to go in couples because it was too threatening to go alone. It was a horrible, creepy place and anyone could hide in any place.

When I thought it was all clear I went to wash Malcolm's hair, but on the way back, as we came up past the cash desk, those men were standing there. They saw me. In a flash, I ran up the stairs. They chased me up the stairs and down the corridor. I took off my sandals to run faster, then flew up the corridor, the stairs, and along more corridors. I reached our door, rushed in, and locked it. I was so scared.

Overall, they came to our door five times. The hotel manager came up. The men told him that the girls were in there, and our "chaperone" said that these men were causing a nuisance. By 11 o'clock they gave up. It must be because Vanessa accepted that ring from one of them and they wanted it back. Frank suggested that accepting a ring may have been like getting engaged.

Day 24   17th October

BEIRUT TO DAMASCUS

This morning I went out to the Money Changers to get a good exchange, and who should I find waiting outside the hotel, but one of these wretched men. I shot back in, in double-quick time, until he had gone. Wandering amongst Arabs in Beirut, alone, with these men hovering about was unnerving, to say the least. Changing money was exciting. We had to go round different money changers, not banks, and they all gave different rates. Some gave particularly good and some poorer.

The porters at the hotel almost snatched our bags away from us, despite our insistence not to, and then tried to force a tip out of us. We left at 10 a.m., There was a crowd of men standing around to see us off.

The journey from Beirut took us past banana plantations, olive groves, cotton fields, date palms, and people working in the fields. Lunch stop was taken in the Beqaa valley, at **Baalbek**, or "Sun" city, where we had time to wander around the ancient ruins of the Temple of Jupiter and the Temple of Bacchus. It was interesting and the view down on the surrounding countryside was good. This was the first place where we saw large, desert-like sandy hills.

The remainder of the journey took us through mountains and hills to **Damascus,** where we arrived after dark and were very tired. The hotel was Hotel Nefertiti and cost me about 5/- bed and breakfast. This evening we went to a restaurant and had a particularly good, five-course, meal for 3/6. By now, I am feeling extremely tired through the travelling, heat, and dysentery.

Day 25   18th October

DAMASCUS

This morning we had a delightful breakfast at hotel Nefertiti; it consisted of omelette, bread and jam, and tea. Afterwards, eight of us, Malcolm, Barry, Bob, Martin, Dorothy, Venessa, Suzanne, and I went to see Damascus. We had not gone far when a boy from the town got talking to Barry and offered to take us to see his factory of copper and silk work. So he got two taxis for us, and we went up the street called Straight and turned into a little, narrow back street, just by the old city gateway, and in the same street was Ananias' house.

We were invited in for tea, and sat in the small courtyard, round a little pond and fountain. Three men entertained us over tea, and one smoked his Hubble-bubble pipe, Malcolm had a go and went green. Later we were told that they exported goods all over the world, and we were shown many beautiful pieces of copper work, both antique and modern, and inlaid woodwork and silks. Copper comes from Japan, and it has to be heated and then hammered out by hand before it can be engraved. There was one large tray that had taken a year to make.

We were also shown the various stages of inlaid woodwork. First small sticks of various woods are tied together in bundles and glued, then allowed to dry in the sun for a few days. Later they are put into the desired designs and fitted together, glued, and pressed, before being cut and polished. Of course, we were encouraged to buy. They were good salesmen. Everyone, except Malcolm and I, bought beautiful brocade work for dresses. The material was handmade and didn't crease, whereas the machine-made material did crease. I bought a doll in national costume and was well satisfied, as I was collecting one from each country, for my collection.

Afterwards, we visited the house of Ananias, which is now a chapel. Inside is the original house, which is below ground, and the chapel contains three pictures of Paul. One blinded, one receiving sight and one being let down by a basket.

Next, we walked through the old Roman archway and into the Street called Straight, then through the covered bazaar. There was a great Eastern atmosphere here. People in national costume riding on donkeys, or leading laden donkeys through the crowds. Corrugated iron, full of holes, formed the roof of the bazaar, but I don't think it would be much use in rainy weather. Men sat by the waysides with heaps of goods around them, such as onions, or fruit, but I can't possibly begin to imagine how they could ever scrape together an existence on their profits. Little children kept coming up and asking for money, and one little fellow followed us back to the hotel, right across Damascus!

We visited a huge mosque, called the Great Umayyad Mosque, and we girls had to wear black flowing cloaks and we all looked as if we were out on parade on graduation day. Secretly I thought that we looked like witches going along without our brooms and cats. The mosque, to me, was not so impressive as the Blue Mosque at Istanbul, but some of the others liked this better. It was unusual, it was certainly very big. Inside was the mausoleum of John the Baptist. This tomb was huge, making it look as if he was a giant.

We bargained, in the market with Martin, who was an expert at this. Next, we visited another mosque, but couldn't go in because it was closed. Then came back to the hotel. **On the way, I saw a Muslim man** praying in the street. They are not ashamed of their religion, and it makes me wonder if some of us Christians are afraid to be "fools for Christ's sake."

After going out for supper. We went back to have a chin wag in the boy's room. Malcolm had a new job for me, and that was to manicure his nails!! I've already spent an evening washing his hair, and another brushing it, but I don't mind. Suddenly **to my surprise he picked up the hotel Bible and began to read to me. First, he read of Christ's birth, then of the creation. He said that the story of creation gives him new hope because if God could make everything in seven days, then surely, he can have the strength and courage for one day. It was lovely to hear him read the Bible.**

The hotel manageress was once a missionary but now has this hotel. She had Bibles in all the rooms. She was concerned about the politics and told me that Syria is becoming communist, that much has to be given to the government, police inspect each hotel, and some people are imprisoned easily. Her sister is in Armenia and is starving because of the strict government. She was very worried. I've learned quite a lot on this trip, I was never interested in politics before.

Day 26   19th October

DAMASCUS TO JERUSALEM

This morning we left Damascus and journeyed out through the flat countryside to the Syria and Jordan frontier. About an hour was spent here. The weather was extremely hot, well into the 90s.

The lunch stop was at **Jerash**, where two hours were spent looking at old Roman columns, streets, and amphitheatre. These ruins are alleged to be the most complete examples of Roman provincial city planning in the Middle East. The Theatre accommodated 5,000 people and the acoustics in the South Theatre was extremely good. The Forum has 56 Ionic columns. There is the Temple of Artemis and Hadrian's Triumphal Arch. The paved colonnaded street is half a mile long.

I sat on the veranda of the restaurant, in the shade, and viewed it all in comfort, because the restaurant was set up on the hilltop and everything could be seen perfectly, and I couldn't see any sense in panting around in such heat.

When we eventually left at 2 p.m., Mr Tulley, the Australian, was taken ill, and we had to stop a car driven by two nuns. We exchanged Mr Tulley for their luggage, and they took him to Amman hospital. It was found that he was dehydrated and had to discontinue the trip and fly the rest of the way with his wife. He was in his eighties. Apparently, this could happen to any of us, if we don't have sufficient water and salt, and if we get too much sun.

On our route from Jericho to Jerusalem, we by-passed the Dead Sea. I saw a group of tents, where people lived, and passed a shepherd, dressed as in olden times, leading his flock of sheep. We went through rugged, rocky areas, and I was reminded that the Bible story of the Good Samaritan was set here. For it was between Jericho to Jerusalem that a man was travelling, when he got beaten up by thieves and left to die until the good Samaritan came along and rescued him.

We stayed in the Regent Hotel, in **Jerusalem,** and the cost for dinner, bed, and breakfast was £1, but tonight we dined at the Ritz hotel because our hotel hadn't prepared for us. It was quite luxurious.

We called at the British Embassy for mail, and I got fourteen letters. When I gave my name, the chap knew it at once. Jerusalem is a clean, tidy place, but the courier warned us single girls about the hospitality of the inhabitants, and told us not to accept any gifts, or offers of any sort.

Day 27   20th October

JERUSALEM

As we had two days in Jerusalem I decided to go on the conducted tour of Jerusalem and Bethlehem. We left by coach at 9a.m., and went up to the Garden of Gethsemane, at the foot of the Mount of Olives. The olive trees are said to be the very ones our Lord saw, and indeed I can well believe it, for they look so huge and ancient. Of the whole tour, this was the one thing that I was able to accept as being genuine, the others were the rock that looked like a skull, where Jesus was crucified and the rock rent in two, although in a glass case, looked genuine.

Everywhere else, churches had been erected around places that related to Jesus. Commercialism ruined the place and stole the religious atmosphere. People were just trying to make money out of it. Even our guide was a Muslim. No matter where we went, people were trying to sell us postcards or film slides or trying to take our photographs in churches. Roger, our courier, had told us that if we went on that tour, and had any sort of faith at all, it would have to be strong to withstand the commercialism, and he was right because several people in our party were shocked at the whole commercial set up.

Mount Calvary was the worst, it was just a rock inside a church with a chapel upstairs above it, whilst the tomb was downstairs in the church. Everything seemed to be so manipulated. Those guides were not Christian and were just making money out of it. Different guides took people to different sites for the same story. I was horrified.

We drove to **Bethlehem,** across arid, rolling hills. and I was comforted to think that the scenery was genuine, and just as our Lord had seen it. We passed people travelling on donkeys and saw a large water pipe that went between Jerusalem and Bethlehem. On the way out of Bethlehem, we were taken into a tourist shop and given free drinks to encourage us to buy.

At Bethlehem we entered The Church of the Nativity, and down in the crypt was the manager. Apparently, Jesus had been born in a cave. Lots of people lived in caves, and some still do, because we passed caves inhabited by Arab refugees from Palestine and Israel. We saw the Shepherds Field.

We returned to Jerusalem. After lunch, we were taken on a tour, by foot, within walled Jerusalem. Here we walked up and down narrow streets and stairs, full of interest and intrigue. Then we visited the 14 stages of the cross, along the Via Dolorosa, or Way of the cross. The Pool of Bethesda is now within the city walls, but at the time of Christ's life on earth, it was outside.

From Jerusalem, we saw the Mount of Olives, the Shepherd's field and places mentioned in the Bible. They were closer to each other and not as big, and distant as I had imagined. Mount Moriah was nearby, and the Valley of Kidron stretched between Jerusalem and the Mount of Olives. With this view behind, a photograph was taken of all the people on the bus. It has made a pleasant souvenir.

After evening dinner, I went to the Bible shop and bought a New Testament for my nephews because it had a cover made from olive wood. The man who sold it to me told me he was Brethren and that a small number of them met in a house, but that the numbers were diminishing because several had emigrated to places like Canada. 6% of Jerusalem are not Muslim, and those who are Christians are united, irrespective of their denomination. Not like in England, where it is a Christian country and people have wasted time causing divisions amongst the denominations. This man was also connected with the Blind Orphanage, and also knows Mr Howley and the Mr Tattford's junior and senior, who were visiting speakers at my home church.

We were told that in Bethlehem 80% of the people are Christians. It was good to walk and see places that our Lord saw, and many people still go about on donkeys, as in His day. **My Bible is now popular on the bus, as many people keep borrowing it, and are interested, and one boy wants to buy his own to read for the rest of the journey.**

Day 28   21st   October

JERUSALEM

This morning Audrey and I visited the Home for Blind Girls in Jerusalem. We caught a local bus at the bus station. Some people squatted on the pavements eating. Men walked by carrying huge trays of food on their heads, and the locals, wearing embroidered clothing, piled on buses.

The principal of the orphanage, who was blind, was a small woman, with an independent, self-reliant air about her, and confidence oozed from her. She made us very welcome and took us to see the girls' preparing olives for pickling.

Children ran around the playground, laughing, with their little hands groping before them, and the girls squatted in a shed banging olives with stones, to get out the juices, ready to pour on salt and lemon juice.

The principal said how the home had raised £8,000 in ten years, on a non-commercial basis, for their new home, and that she had just paid the first instalment.

In the course of conversation, it turned out that, one of her teachers was Ruth Fiddler's friend, Grace, who I met in 1959, at our chapel, when she spent Christmas with them. It was nice meeting her.

After leaving this cool house, we went out into the blazing sun, to catch a bus back. A bus was coming, and we hopped on. It was a real boneshaker. I sat just inside the door, and as it tore up the road, every time it swerved to avoid a car, I nearly fell off my seat and had to hang on to stay on the bus.

In the afternoon Audrey and I went to the market. I bought a box of cheese costing 60 fils and gave the chap 100 fils, but my 40 fils change didn't appear.

After he had served another customer I asked him for my change, but he just turned away and ignored me. When I pressed the subject, another chap came up, and he also grinned and pretended not to understand, although both had been talking perfect English before. So, getting fed up with this, I just opened the till, took out the change, and showed them, whereupon they showed signs of understanding. In the evening, after dinner, we walked down to see the shops.

Frank and Beryl got engaged.

WEEK FIVE

Day 29   22nd October

JERUSALEM TO PETRA

This morning we had a late start from Jerusalem and left about 9.30 a.m. The temperature today, and over the past few days, has been over 90 degrees and is only just bearable. We took the road out to Jericho.

Jericho is like an oasis in the desert, with lush palm trees, and greenery growing near the Jordan. Part of Jericho has numerous Arab refugee houses, for refugees from Israel. Every other Arab country has absorbed its quantity of refugees, into the normal population, but **Jordan** has not. In Jericho, we saw the excavations of the old walls. Jericho has a history spanning 9,000 years and is the world's oldest city discovered.

From here, we went to the **river Jordan** and saw the place where Christ was baptized or the alleged place. The river Jordan has dried up a lot since Bible times but is still muddy. It was fast-flowing, and I could quite understand Naaman's objection to having to dip in it seven times, it looked horrible and most unwelcoming.

Our next stop was, at the **Dead Sea,** for a swim. It is the lowest spot on earth, being some 1,300 feet below sea level. It was midday and the sun was beating down. I thought we were quite mad to go swimming in such heat, but I just couldn't miss that opportunity.   It was a funny feeling trying to get my feet to go down onto the ground, and swimming on the front was a joke, because the feet and seat rise too high in the water, making it impossible to do breaststroke because the legs and feet just won't stay under the water. Anyway, it was a good laugh, even though the water did taste vile, and stung the eyes terribly. We have been told to drink plenty of water and to take plenty of salt in the hot climates, but I reckon I had my quota of salt in one go!! My skin felt briny and slimy with salt, but afterwards, it was nice to have a shower in freshwater.

We visited the Qumran caves where the Dead Sea Scrolls were discovered. In this area are several caves which have been excavated for finds. The view across the Dead Sea to Mount Nebo was beautiful. This was where Moses viewed the Promised Land, and we saw the Mount of Temptation, where Satan tried to tempt Jesus, without success.

The journey in the afternoon took us to **Amman,** and then on across absolute desert for 350 miles to **Petra**, we arrived at 11 p.m., where we slept the night, camping in the hotel foyer. Accommodation ranged from 6d to £2.

Day 30   23rd October

PETRA TO AMMAN

This morning we were awakened at 5 am, and left at
7.15 a.m. to go to Petra, the "rose-red city, half as old
as time". Magnificent and mysterious, it is hidden in
the mountains and is approached through a very narrow
passage known as the Siq Gorge. Some by horse and
some on foot, we set off to see the ancient cave city.
This gorge was beautiful, pink coloured rocks, and
opened out to carved tombs, temples, and houses.
Carved in such a way that the yellow, white, mauve and
pink graining in the rocks showed up beautifully. It was
the centre of the Nabatean Arabs whose nobility were
buried in tombs cut from the rock.

Very few people still live in these caves. We met a
woman squatting on the ground, sorting over bits of
pottery, and there, sitting in the dust next to her was a
little 5-month-old girl dressed in black. She looked the
sweetest little thing, with long curling eyelashes, but
flies kept alighting on her tiny face.

Our guide was a bombastic type of person, who
should have been on the stage, and he informed us that
the tombs were carved in either 1 AD or 1BC. Gill and
I had hired a horse between us. After walking there and
looking around, it was my turn to come back by horse.
It was the first time I had ever been on a horse, and I
felt so high up there, that when the horse turned round
to start off, I nearly shot over the side. When I got off,
after riding for an hour, it was even funnier, for I just
couldn't figure out how to get off, and ended up with
the horse leader helping me, but I slipped off and
underneath the horse!!   I felt such an idiot, with all

those horse-riding men gazing down at me in astonishment.

We ate our picnic lunch in the hotel. We must have been like a whirlwind to the proprietors because we purchased practically nothing, and then left. It was so hot in Petra. After lunch, we set off in the coach for Amman. The journey was about 350 miles across the desert. The first 40 miles were hilly, and we stopped to get water from the spring of Moses' rock, and then the remainder was across the flat, arid, brown desert. All there was to see was the occasional Bedouin tent, or an Arab riding his camel, horse, or donkey. The clouds gathered and the wind got up, causing whirlwinds, and dust storms, in several places. Just before we arrived in Amman, a beautiful rainbow formed, and the ends seemed to sink into the earth.

Amman, the capital of Jordan, is built on hills and is not very impressive. The houses blend with the colour of the soil, which is very monotonous to see. In fact, I, am tired of the desert colour altogether, and we've only just begun, but that's because I don't like brown colours. At one shop in Amman, meat was hanging outside and before buying it the purchasers were handling and mauling it about to see if it was suitable for them. No wonder people get illnesses and with a lack of refrigerated conditions I'm sure half the meat must go rotten before the sale.

Nearly everyone on the bus now has, or has had, stomach upsets of one sort or another. Now, I find the journey very tiring, although extremely interesting. I am, however, tired of Roman amphitheatres and remains, because we have seen a lot in the past month, and my brain has reached the point where it can't absorb any more of that type of history.

At first, I was fascinated by Arabs and their way of life, but now I am bored with having to look round every corner before going by, and of being touched, pinched, and knocked into, every time I set foot outside the bus. Tired also of hearing Eastern music wailing, of hearing the Imam call the people to prayer, of looking at scraggy, smelly little shops, with just pull-down shutters, which separates them from the street at night, and of hearing beggars muttering for money. Most of all I find it waring to have to bargain for everything.

It was fun at first but really when you have to bargain over necessities for food, goods, and even for hotel accommodation, and to constantly check that I am not being short-changed. I got a bit fed up with it. It was too much effort. What with the heat and everyone being ill with dysentery, I thought, "Oh, to be in England!"

It should be valuable to look back upon. It makes me even more appreciative of my home, where I know that every night, I am going to get a bed, and every day a satisfying meal, and where there is safety in going out, and shopping is easy, and everywhere is beautiful and green.

Day 31   24th October

AMMAN TO RUT BAH WELLS

Several of us had found our own hotels in Amman, and this morning we did not get time for a proper breakfast, or rather, we could not find anywhere that sold it. Instead, we ate blancmange in an ice cream shop.

We travelled along the oil pipeline road that links Jordan with Iraq. This part of the Great Syrian Desert is a wilderness of black basalt rock and volcanic debris. So the journey was unusual, across the black, bleak desert with nothing to look at, except a vast expanse of sand, and nothing at all on the horizon. I had been told that the desert would be sticky and hot, and most uncomfortable, but today there was a thunderstorm, and the sky was overcast, so the air was cool. Whoever would have imagined pouring rain and slippery, sludgy mud to walk on, in the desert?

After a few hours driving, we came to **H4** at the **Iraq border**, which used to be an old English military station. This was a place of all places! All that was there were about half a dozen wooden and mud shacks, with verandas, and rooves made of reed. Lorries and cars were waiting, together with a jeep of English people, who looked tired out and ill. There had been eleven of them to start with, but the company had now dwindled to six. Five boys and one girl.

At the border, we spent our last odd coins on tea and a sandwich, which we had sitting under a leaky grass roof, outside a shack. The sandwich was tasty if you didn't stop to think about it. It was prepared in a stall, which, I am sure if the sun was shining, would have been fly-infested. The bread was a flat unleavened roll, cut open, and stuffed with cucumber, meat, greenery, and tomato. Probably all unwashed too, but when you are famished, it doesn't do to think of such things. Later we went across to a little shop, and one of the girls asked the owner where there was a toilet in the vicinity, whereupon he answered that he did not know, so goodness knows what he did.

After the afternoon drive from H4, the border town, to **Rut bah Wells**, we stayed here the night. All that was there were a few houses and a hotel, and then a little further away was our rest house.

There was nothing to see, except flat desert, lit up under the full moon, which was brightly shining, with a large circle around. It looked beautiful. Dogs barked, and howled, in the distance, and it was eerie. The guest house was scruffy and dull. Concrete walls and corridors made it appear unwelcoming. We stayed here "native style", which meant, no toilet paper, towels, soap, or clean linen. We slept in beds that other people had used, so had dirty bed linen, but it was cheap.

Day 32   25th October

RUT BAH WELLS TO BAGHDAD

This morning we got up, just after 4 a.m. to leave at
5 a.m. Personally, I think we left in the dark so that we
couldn't see the horrid surroundings where we had
slept. The one good thing about the place was the
electric fan, which we had on all night to keep us cool.
On waking in the morning, I got up, dressed, and
wandered up the corridor to wash at the only tap. We
were not alone as early risers, for two Arab ladies
hurried along the corridor, with long black gowns
flowing, and we all met at this tap.

Today's journey was varied. The first part crossed
the flat barren desert, but after four, or five, hours'
drive, we came to the **River Euphrates** and stopped at
a European-style hotel for tea and sandwiches. One
tomato sandwich cost 2/-. After the arid desert, this
valley around the Euphrates was certainly an oasis, it
was lovely and green, with palm trees growing by pools
of water. We are now in the land between the two rivers
of Mesopotamia, the Euphrates, and the river Tigris,
where one of the world's oldest civilizations began.
The ancient Sumerians of this region regarded its lush
vegetation as the original site of the Garden of Eden.

Continuing through this fertile area, we came to
Babylon, or its remains, for nothing but a few odd ruins
are left. Excavation is still taking place, and some of
the findings are shown in a museum within the
reconstructed city gates. Babylon itself was a great
disappointment, for the hanging gardens are nothing to
look at. Only mud clay foundations remain. One or two
walls were well preserved and showed horses, made in
relief from raised mud on the bricks. I remembered that

the Bible gave an account of the destruction of Babylon, so later looked it up. Gods' wrath for their disobedience to Him, and His prophecy that the place would be destroyed and never rebuilt, certainly came true. We spent an hour or so walking amongst bits of pottery. Guards kept chasing us away, telling us that they were not original. They must have been because surely no one had been scattering modern pottery about.

One of our party, was an ageing professor, from Auckland University. His subject was history, and although he found the Holy Land and other ancient places, of great interest, he did get fed up when people asked him about their history, and he snapped back at times, "Why don't you read it up for yourselves? I did." He got so cross with the journey that he ended up flying home from Baghdad.

We got back on the bus and continued our journey to **Baghdad**. Baghdad is situated on the **River Tigris**, in a fertile area. It is a large modern city that is quite spread out. The bus stopped in the main square and several of us got out to find our own hotels. Eventually, we found a reasonably priced place and took a three-bedroom, for four, which cost about 6/- each. This was quite comfortable. Two beds were put together for three to sleep on. That evening Sue, Dot, Vanessa, Barry, and I went out for dinner. The recommended hotel was situated down by the river, but as it was charging 10/- for tea and sandwich, we decided against it. We were on a tight budget. Anyway, it did not look as good as the Thames and smelt far worse, so we found somewhere else and had egg and chips, how British can you get!! Coffee in our room and a chat rounded off the day.

Day 33   26th October

BAGHDAD TO
IRAQ BORDER RETURN TO BAGHDAD

This morning we left at 7 a.m. for the Iraqi and Iran border, 150 miles away. It took quite a while for us to get out of Baghdad because the streets were not well signposted and also, we had to find a diesel pump for the bus. Eventually, we found it, but the street it was in was flooded, because of the heavy rain of the four previous days. The men pumping away the water didn't seem to have much idea, and this brought home to us the haphazard way of going about things in Iraq.

No one trusts anyone, the police don't trust the government and the government doesn't trust the army, so because of this, and the constant change of government, there are many check posts in Iraq. We travel a few miles and then get stopped, for someone to come in and look at passports, or to count us. Overall, it is far from being an efficiently run country. Poverty and beggars abound, and no one seems to be getting much done in a lot of things, such as hygiene. I am not surprised that cholera sweeps the place at times.

The ride to the frontier took about four hours. On the way, we all had to get out of the bus, while it was manoeuvred over a humpback railway road. The bus cleared the road by a mere fraction of an inch, also we went through a flooded road, and it looked for all the world as if we were fording a river.

At the frontier, we spent up our last odd coins on glasses of tea, tins of food, and packets of biscuits, and then sat down to wait. After waiting here two or three hours our coach went to the Iran border to see if they would allow us to enter because the Iraqi border wouldn't clear us until we had permission to enter into Iran. This was supposed to be due to the cholera outbreak.

The reply came back that we could not go through, because there was cholera in Iraq, and no word had been received from Tehran to open the border, as it was the Shah's birthday, and therefore a public holiday, and also because his birthday was followed by religious holidays. The Embassy in Baghdad had told us that the border was now open, subject to 48 hours in quarantine, but the actual border had not received official instructions. After waiting five hours, it was a case of, "You go away and take your germs with you." So we had to go back to Baghdad.

Everyone was downhearted about this because we did not like Baghdad, and also it put us behind in our schedule, and we wondered how much of the trip we would have to leave out in order to get to Bombay on time for the boat. We were originally supposed to have one complete day in Baghdad but had missed this out in case there was trouble at the border, and it was a good job we did.

I sent a postcard of Baghdad, home to my family saying,
" What a filthy, stinking, dirty hovel that is too. I can't understand you liking it Dad. It must have altered since you were here. These men keep pinching and poking, and they spit everywhere. How they ever earn a living just sitting all day in the dirt by old tyres or pots and pans, I'll never know. There's one place I never want to visit again and that's this scruffy old land.It's interesting but just squalor."

Back at Baghdad, and installed in our hotels, we discovered that Indiaman was in town. This is a rival company to Penn, which does the same route to India.

They had almost booked the place out. In the evening we went to a nice cheap place for a shish -kebab and then went up the road to get real fruit juice.

I am tired of coffee, sweet or strong, black tea, and cola drinks. They are all so sweet that they do not quench the thirst, but the drinks squeezed from oranges and pomegranates, taken straight from the fridge, are delicious, refreshing, and nourishing. On the way back to the hotel we met some of the Indiaman crowd and compared notes. They have been held up for three days through engine trouble.

Day 34   27th October

BAGHDAD

Today we had a free day in Baghdad, so after having
breakfast in bed, which consisted of eggs, bread, and
tea, we went out to wander down the streets of Baghdad
with mud everywhere, as the floods subsided. They had
had storms for three days. Actually, as we crossed the
desert, there was thunder, lightning, and heavy rain,
and I could not help feeling how lucky we were to have
cool weather, in that unprotected barren place. It was
hot in Baghdad, but no hotter than other places we had
been to. The temperature had been well up in the 90s
for about three weeks now and I have a lovely tan, and
my hair is getting fairer. I have a form of dysentery
which I have had for a couple of weeks, so the weight
is just falling off me, which I don't mind, now my green
dress is loose on me.

Gill wanted to trace a friend, so we started by going
to the British Embassy, where, as outside all British
embassies so far, we found GB cars doing similar trips
to ourselves. On the way, two Arab university students
attached themselves to us and offered to show us
around Baghdad. They said that they wanted to practise
their English.

We went on a rowing boat across the Tigris River
to the market. The jewellery section was a bit scruffy
and smelly but had silver and gold displayed in small,
lock-up glass top tables. The place smelt of lavatories,
and drains, and was completely unpleasant in its
surroundings of derelict buildings.

Old Baghdad is famed for its tiled buildings and
silks. We walked further through the market, past silks,
and materials to household wares, and then writing

books. In the market was an entrance to an old university, and many students went to buy books and pens.

Our guides told us that there was somewhere else they wanted us to see. We had no idea what they had in mind, but, as they were so pleasant, we trusted them, and were lulled into going with them. They made a phone call, then hailed a taxi, which took us to the other side of Baghdad. Past dome-shaped mosques, and large, luxurious dwellings, along a wide main road, out of town along a desert track to a little cafe. Here a man was waiting. We were introduced and invited inside.

The boys went, leaving us sitting at a table with this much older man. We did question where they were going, and they said they would be coming back. So we felt assured and waited with this stranger, who was their friend.

The dingy cafe was the usual filthy, fly-infested, little place, bug-ridden, and horrible. Unexpectedly, lunch was brought out. I watched, in horror, as I thought about each item as it was placed on the table. First came salad that, if washed at all, was washed in water full of germs, and I could see little creatures crawling about the tomatoes and cucumber. We had been advised not to eat these because the vegetables suck up sewer water, and we could get ill. Then flat, hard, unleavened bread arrived and was slapped down on our dirty table. Flies walked across it. I wondered if it had been served up several times before to other people.

Then came shish kebab. The thought of eating meat in these countries is repulsive because it hangs up outside the shops, rotting in the heat, with no refrigeration, in the most unhygienic conditions. Flies walk over it. Dust blows up and customers handle it. Anyway, we ate the meal. We were given water to drink, and you never, never drink water, but what could we do? We were dying of thirst and starving hungry, and we did not want to offend the chap.

Afterwards, I wished I had offended him because blow me down if he did not start bargaining with the café owner. The restaurant owner came out and the two men argued loudly, then went back into the kitchen. I asked our host why they were arguing. He told us that he wanted to buy us and offered £1,000 each. I laughed, thinking it was a joke, and could visualize my parents with a camel in the garden, and me out there as a slave doing housework. I had no idea!

We were very apprehensive of him after this, particularly as his other colleagues, our guides, had disappeared. When I realised it was true, I got up and said, "Come on Gill." She got up. With that, the whole mood changed. Our host leapt up from the table and the boys reappeared. Everyone turned aggressive and we were rushed outside where a private car was waiting driven by yet another friend.

The men forced us to get in the car and the boys disappeared. We asked the driver what was going on and he told us that the café owner used to buy girls in the Slave Market. Then three men got in and so now we were outnumbered. There wasn't much we could do about the situation because we were out in a very lonely spot, and we didn't know where, in Baghdad, we were, nor how to get back. So the best thing was to go with these men, in their car, and hope for the best.

We said we wanted to go back to our hotel in Baghdad. None of it. They took us way, way out. I was furious and scared. We demanded to be taken back. It was no joke when there were four Arabs all chatting away in their language. Years and years older than us and what did they want with two young white girls, after they had already tried to sell us off, or someone tried to buy us. We were not at all happy about this.

Quickly, we were speeding out of Baghdad. We kept insisting that they take us back to the centre, only to be told that Baghdad was a big place and that we were still in it. Through the back window, I could see the desert dust swirling up behind us and watched the minarets of Baghdad getting smaller and smaller until they disappeared on the horizon, and we were far away in the desert. We were not going back. We were travelling in the opposite direction, away from Baghdad. It was terrifying.

We told them to stop and let us out, but they refused and went even faster. I opened the door to jump out but could see that it was far too dangerous to jump, we were going too fast. We would get injured and how could we get across the desert to go back by foot? We were helpless and in their control. There was no escape. I just prayed that God would protect us and help us.

Soon, we were far away, at a casino, which, had a lovely garden. It was like an oasis. They told us that there were beautiful girls inside, and they wanted us to meet them. The grass was soft and spongy, streams trickled through the flower-strewn garden. Frogs jumped in the water. There was not sufficient shade to sit outside, so I sat back in the car watching. They tried all the doors and windows, rattled, and shook them but could not get an answer. They scratched their heads and talked together. They had not expected this, so they decided not to stay. I told them to take us back to Baghdad. After a bit of argument, we got our way. We were no use to them apart from being like cargo that was worth money, and the purchaser was not there.

We were relieved to be taken back, but even on the way, they kept detouring, to hang out the time. First, we saw a monument, then a suspension bridge, then they began to head out of town again. We, however, kept an eye open for the right way, and I kept telling them when they changed course, so they did not get far in making off with us. They were probably hoping that someone would contact them, and they would go back with us. They were astonished at my sense of direction, but that is one of my gifts, and I made use of it.

Once out of the car, we looked at each other with a sigh of relief. That was a narrow escape. Our first thought was to get a nice, cool refreshing fruit drink from a little shop nearby. I have never known such thirst before. That drink of cold, squashed oranges was absolutely wonderful.

I will pause my story for a moment as this is an appropriate place to include a newspaper report which my father cut from The Times newspaper March 1967 referring to 1966. I had no idea that such things were going on, and I never read this report until long after I was back home in England. It tells of what was happening near to where I was, and, in the area, we were in.

"SLAVES AS SAUDI "STATUS SYMBOL"
"The wealth produced in Saudi Arabia by oil royalties has converted slaves into status symbols, and "slaves are sold openly in the markets," according to a memorandum submitted to Mohammed Awad, the special United Nations rapporteur on slavery, by the British Anti-Slavery Society. In Riyadh the capital, "slaves are taken around following their dealer in yokes like cattle, six or seven at a time," he said. A report prepared by Mr Awad presents the replies by 76 members of the United Nations to his questionnaire, asking if slavery, the slave trade, or practices similar to slavery existed on their territory. His report is

scheduled for consideration by the Human Rights Commission this week, New York Times News Service."

To continue my story: -

At about 4 p.m. we went by our bus to see Ctesiphon. Here a little encampment of people existed, who lived in mud houses, and we were invited to have a glass of coffee in their chi house. This was about one mouthful of coffee in a handle-less cup, which was never washed between drinks. I reckon we drank more bugs than coffee.

The Arch of Ctesiphon is the largest, unsupported, mud-brick arch, in the world. It was built hundreds of years ago, it is thought, between the third and sixth century, and was a trading centre along the old Silk Road. Now only a ruin remains. I sat gazing at it, recalling stories told to me by my father, about his time here, when in the Royal Naval Air Service at the end of the First World War. He said that some dare-devil pilots used to fly through that arch in their bi-wing planes. Now I was watching the birds flying beneath that arch and perching on the top. There was an aura of calm as I listened to those birds singing and watched the sunset on that serene summer evening. As the golden sun rays spread across the sky, the arch became a silhouette of beauty. Relaxing peace and stillness was like a breath of fragrant air.

I sat alone reflecting on what had happened. We had been lulled into a feeling of false security by the friendliness of the boys. We had been trapped, like insects caught on a spider's web. In a situation of helplessness, where we could not escape. Powerless. The trauma and terror seemed to refrigerate and numb the brain.

My thoughts turned to home, and I wondered what they would be doing. Before I left England, the people at my church promised to pray for me regularly, that God would keep me safe. When I worked out the time difference, between England and Baghdad, I realised that their prayer meeting was taking place at the exact time, that we were being taken to that brothel. **Amazing. The power of prayer and God's protection.**

I felt warm tranquillity of peace and calm refill me, as my brain thawed from its fearful, frozen state. As evening drew on, the mosquitoes began to bite, so we left in the coach, remembering Ctesiphon with her ancient grinding wheel and settlement. In the evening we went to our shish kebab shop to eat, and then back to the hotel.

Day 35   28th October

BAGHDAD TO IRAN BORDER

This morning, after breakfast in bed, we left early for the border. Tea was fabulous with condensed milk, which made such a change from the usual strong, sweet, sickly tea, that I now find quite indigestible. The route to the border was just the same as before, except that the floods had subsided. We arrived at the Iraq border at 11 a.m. in anticipation of entry into Iran. Several Iraqi and Iranian people were already there, sitting patiently. We joined them and sat inside the customs house, out of the intense, baking heat, which poured down ruthlessly. We hung around waiting for over six hours.

Women sat on the floor feeding tiny babies under their black robes. Men sat outside in the shade of the building cooking shish kebabs, and old men sat in groups, spitting, and smoking. Dogs and puppies sprawled about in the shade with insufficient energy to wag their tails, until apple peel, or cheese tinfoil was thrown down. Then they all suddenly revived to pounce and devour the lot, including the tinfoil and paper. Their ribs showed through their mangy coats. I expect they only lived on scraps. It was a case of survival of the fittest, as puppies strove with dogs in the competition.

Soon an English Rover arrived, and the owner got everyone moving. While we were still trying to get through the border, he had got everyone organized, and was thanking people profusely, bowed and scraped and disappeared over the border. I discovered later that he was a high official in the diplomatic service at Tehran, but he still suffered quarantine for nearly as long as us.

After this, some of us went up onto a little hill and sat in the sun enjoying a slight breeze. We lay there reading, chatting, and just looking, gazing out across the desert hills, and vast expanse of sky. It was really beautiful watching the sun going down and seeing the rosy sky casting a pink-purple hue onto these hills until everywhere was calm and reddish, under the fading sky and decreasing heat. It was really a most inspiring sight.

Suddenly our bus returned from the border, hooting furiously on its usual loud, two-toned horn. Then we knew that we were going to be allowed into Iran. Everyone jumped up, with joy, and made for the bus, and we went down the road, about a half a mile, to the Iran border. This time, Rodger had a copy of the official telegram, from the Embassy, instructing the border to open up for us, but nothing quite so simple.

We were only allowed into quarantine on the condition that we took our own food, and provided we had our own beds and tents. We had already stocked up with tins, in expectation of this, and tents, we told the officials, was English for sleeping bags, because we could get in them. So we were allowed in. However, there was only one building there, which was already full of Iranians, so we had to camp out under the stars. We were ushered into a small compound, surrounded by barbed wire, and allotted a patch, on which to pitch our camp beds. Where we spent 48 hours. Daytime was extremely hot, over 100 degrees, and night-time was not too cold, except just before dawn, when it was really chilly.

Toilet and washing facilities consisted of half a dozen holes in sheds, on either side of the building, where water jugs and taps acted as flushing systems. Outside these toilets was placed one cold tap, and water poured into a large puddle, which got increasingly full of soap, toothpaste, and scum. Inside the building was a shower, and a similar styled toilet to outsides, except it, was tiled.

In the evening we purchased a meal of rice and meat and sat drinking coffee, and Canada Dry lemonade. At 9.30 p.m. an official ordered us to bed, and armed men patrolled the fencing when the gates were locked. Although there were gates, we were forbidden to pass through them, all the time we were there. So for two days and nights, we just lazed about chatting. It was great fun sleeping out under the sky. The moon was full, and we lay there watching it move across the sky and the numerous shooting stars shoot across the heavens. Everywhere looked bright in the moon's silver sheen.

WEEK SIX

Day 36   29th October

IRANIAN BORDER

I was awakened by the warmth of the sun as it crept up over the mountain. It shed its full heat on us at about 8.30 a.m. It was really too hot to lay any longer in a down sleeping bag. The only solution was to have breakfast, which was easy, because I only had to stretch out my arm, and there it was beside me. Get up and dress, or rather dress, then get up, which was difficult. As soon as everyone was up, we quickly improvised a shelter, from the exhausting heat, which was
103 degrees, by constructing tents from our stretcher beds and sleeping bags. This was a brilliant idea, we thought until the wind blew some down. Eventually, we discovered a better way of making the tent stay steady, then we just lay around and relaxed.

One lady on our bus was English, and she had travelled so much throughout her life, that she now found it impossible to stop. In fact, she had put her son into boarding school so that her constant wanderings did not interfere with his studies.

There was another, fascinating, lady from Australia, she came laden down with pots and pans, and wore them strung around her neck. She insisted on cooking most, if not all, of her own food, and took great precautions over making sure that all water was really purified. When we eventually reached the desert, she was disgusted with people for not putting their school science into practice. She muttered and chastised everyone who questioned her about why she was digging a hole in the desert, and burying all her food, in saucepans. "Surely you know how to improvise a fridge!!" she snapped in disgust. My camp bed was beside hers and I found her chatter very entertaining.

Today we were tested for cholera, and what a laugh. We all queued up at a table and each given a swab stick. One person lost his cotton wool, another broke the stick, a few couldn't understand where to put it, and several others didn't know what was happening at all. We were all dosed up with antibiotic pills to kill off any germs we may have contracted.

In the evening we had a similar meal to yesterday and then sat listening to a Dutch fellow playing his piano accordion. He used to be in a band that played Slavonic music on TV. He taught us a suitable dance to do to this music, and we had a good time. A Japanese journalist joined us, he has been travelling for five years in a car and has his route painted on the bonnet. At 9.30 p.m. a guard ordered us all to bed. The gates were locked, and men, armed with guns, patrolled again.

There was such a contrast between now and before. These two days have been absolute bliss, just not having to go out, because we were not allowed. To me, they have been, two of the best on the trip, so far. Just lazing around. After five hectic weeks of getting up early, one morning leaving at 5 a.m., and now resting in peace and quiet. Travelling so much, in extreme heat. This was the rest we craved. These days have been restful. Just recovering. After nerve-racking, squalid conditions, now relaxing in tranquillity. After arriving tired at destinations, because we'd been travelling so long, now compelled to stay put and recover. This rest restored us all.

An Evening News Reporter wrote this in an English newspaper.

"TOURISTS FROM BRITAIN HELD AT FRONTIER"

"45 British tourists, 24 of them women, on their way by road to India, have been stranded for nearly a week on the Iraq-Iran frontier, owing to a cholera outbreak in Iraq, says reports reaching London.

They are having to stay in a fortress that is in constant danger of attack by Kurds. The fortress is barricaded after dark, and there are no electricity or sanitary arrangements.

The tourists all have international certificates of vaccination against cholera which the Iranian authorities refuse to accept. There are no quarantine arrangements, and visitors are not told on entering Iraq that all roads out of the country have been closed for at least three months. The average age of the party is 24, The members include nurses, students, engineers, and teachers."

Day 37   30th October

IRANIAN BORDER TO TEHRAN

Today was similar to yesterday, and we were dosed up with more antibiotics. These were not a lot of use, as they were part of a course which we wouldn't complete, but it was a gesture on the Persians part.

In the afternoon, officials told us we could go, as no one had cholera, and we had been in quarantine for 48 hours. They rushed us out in the baking heat. It was 3 p.m. in the afternoon, with the temperature well over 100 degrees. They wanted us to leave fast because there was a queue of people waiting to go into quarantine. We spent about an hour at the Iran border, where they refused to return all our passports without an argument. Eventually, we were allowed to pass into Iran.

We were off. Time had to be made up, so we drove through the night to **Tehran**. We bypassed Kermanshah, where we were supposed to stay, but where we wouldn't have been allowed out, anyway, because of the Kurds. Kermanshah was an oil refining town set high up among the Zagros Mountain peaks.

On Mount Behistun, in Kermanshah Province, we saw where Darius the Great carved his autobiography on a rock. When deciphered, it was an important key to long-forgotten languages. This is now a UNESCO World Heritage site.

As we climbed over the mountain passes, so it became colder and colder in the coach. It got so cold that we all climbed into our sleeping bags and slept, looking like green caterpillars.

Snow-capped the mountain ranges, and it was freezing cold at night. We were fortunate because there was a full moon, which lit the night and made shadows and light appear on the mountains. The mountains shone in grandeur, and little villages stood out clearly. Lights from houses, which nestled together in isolated places, could be seen from a long way off. Everywhere looked so attractive and mystically beautiful.

At 10 a.m. we stopped for tea and then, every two hours after, we stopped at chi shops and went into the warm, little stone buildings half asleep. They were full of men. Goodness knows what they were doing, sitting up drinking tea at those unearthly hours. Maybe they slept in the day when it was too hot. We travelled through the area where there were Kurds.

Once more we watched the sky redden, and glow with the golden sun as the morning broke.

letter 30 October 1966 Iraq/Iran border
"What a difference compared to Iraq. Iran is so civilized, neat, and tidy, even the expressions on the people's faces were more trustworthy. You know, life out here in the Middle East is so vastly different from at home. I could never have imagined that people carried on in such a manner, or lived in such conditions, or led such a way of life as they do here if I had not come to see it. No amount of reading travel books or listening to other people's experiences could ever have convinced me that the middle east was like this.

To start with, you can't buy or get anything without a long session of bargaining. We bargain over the price of food, not only in the markets but in the shops as well. We bargain over hotel accommodation, there are eight of us, four boys and four girls, plus a few others, but us eight always stick together, and we go to find our own hotels at night, because it is so much cheaper, and we always have to do a lot of bargaining and shopping around to get the price down, otherwise we would be fleeced drastically. We bargain over the price of food and drinks, of whether hot showers are included in the cost of bed and breakfast, in fact, there isn't much left that isn't bargained for. I even bargain with money changers to get a better rate.

I fail to see how some Arabs ever make an existence just selling bits of rubbish from dirty squat little shops. Their shops are nothing like ours, with glass fronts. All theirs consist of are a small space with a shuttered front and no backroom or anything, so one often sees them eating and drinking in the street.

The dirt and dust blow into them and coat everything because half the time their pavements are only earth or holey and cracked concrete. Men here cough and spit germs that people can pick up when the dust dries and blows, also they don't use handkerchiefs, instead, they blow their noses through their fingers onto the ground. They think we are dirty blowing into handkerchiefs, wrapping it up, and putting it in our pockets. Customs are different, aren't they? Well, I think I must have given you the impression that I don't like Iraq much".

Day 38   31st October

TEHRAN

We eventually arrived in Tehran at 7a.m. The backdrop of Tehran's main street is a range of mountains, with Mount Demavend, as the pinnacle, reaching 19,000 feet up above sea level. The first port of call was the British Embassy to collect our mail. Then my trouble began. There were six letters for me, but my letter from Clair, containing £10, was not there.

In 1966, the amount of money that we were allowed to take out of England was restricted to a total of £50 to spend in non- Stirling countries, and £250 in Stirling countries, which was taken as travellers' cheques. This was the reason I had to travel on a shoestring, to allow that small amount of money to spread across all the countries I visited.

My friend Clair was working in Iran, so I gave her £10 to take back with her to change into local currency for me, and she was going to give it to me when I met her in Tehran.

Claire wrote to me in Jerusalem to say that she couldn't meet me in Teheran, after all, because it was the Shah's birthday, and lots of others of his family too, so there have been celebrations for about ten days, and holidays. Consequently, she was unable to travel from Kharg island, as she was teaching, and said she would send the money to the Embassy and that it would be waiting there.

The next move was to seek out a hotel. After leaving our goods at the Saadi Hotel, which cost 8/- for bed, we went for breakfast. Somehow or other I managed to lose the others when I went to the bank to change money, and not much wonder either, for they kept me in there half an hour, asked for my passport, which I handed to them displaying British clearly, then the man returned it to me and asked me if I was America or German. Next, I went to money changers for money.

Persia is really great to look at with coloured lights and flags everywhere. I overheard one Iranian saying that everybody loves the Shah, and that the Shah loves his people, and that they place him next to God in position.

I went across the road to the Embassy, once more, as the registry department was open, but no, they didn't have any record of my letter either. So the Embassy sent me to the Consul, who said they hadn't got it but would look.

I was not surprised. It was a bit of a risk to take, anyway, hoping to receive money through the post. The security at the Embassy gate was disgusting, and they think my money was stolen because letters were left in alphabetical order in pigeonholes, in an open-fronted building, just inside the gate, so anyone could help themselves. No one questioned who you were looking through the post and taking it away. No passports were asked for, and nothing had to be signed for. I was determined to phone Clare, as I wasn't going to see her. I asked at the consul where the telephone exchange was. They sent me for a walk half a mile away, where I discovered the exchange, which, when I went in, was packed to capacity. I had visions of me sitting waiting all day, or more, for my call through to Kharg Island. It was no easy matter to phone. In total it took me five hours. I think this was an exciting day.

At first, I went in and asked a man where I could make a call through to Kharg, and he sent me to the end desk, who sent me upstairs, who sent me down to the right-hand desk, who sent me to the left desk, who sent me to another man who said that I couldn't call from there, but would have to go to the Iranian Oil Company, as they were the only people with a direct line through.

The man was in the midst of telling me where to get a taxi, and he even wrote the address down in Persian, but I told him that I couldn't read it, so he wrote it in English as well, when a man offered to take me there in his car, as he was going that way.

I wasn't sure whether to accept or not but decided that I stood as good a chance of getting there in his car, as in a taxi, so I went, and I was jolly glad I did because he really put himself out for me. He was a nice kind man who could hardly speak English but drove me all around Tehran, and he was very good to me.

The Oil Company was at the other end of Tehran. It was a large 15 story building. I expected him to drop me off here, but no, he took me up to the 13th floor and searched for the correct room. At last, we found it, and went in, and he chatted to a man in Persian, who said that I couldn't phone there as they didn't have a line through to Kharg either, but that I would have to go to another office where one of the chief men of the Oil Company was. This man even took me there, parked his car, enquired of lots of people the way, and we went up in a lift. When we got out, they were reconstructing the building, and bits of wire, concrete, and bricks lay everywhere. Well, I would have given up, in fact, I would never have got this far because I can't speak the language, but he found a glass door and went through to a corridor with lots of doors.

After trying every door and finding them locked, we went down into the street again, where we enquired and found that siesta time was from 12 to 4 p.m., it was just after 12. I thanked him and was prepared to find my own way back to the hotel, but he insisted on taking me out to lunch. I thought he had been kind enough without this, but he was bent on doing so. We went to a restaurant in a basement and had rice, butter, and raw egg mixed together. The egg was served in its shell with just the top off, shish kebab, and this time it was more like steak. On the table was a milk bottle, and I was invited to have some, how I wish I hadn't. It was fizzy milk, tasting like Brylcreem, and it made me feel ill all next day, so I didn't eat for nearly 30 hours. It was vile.

From here we went back to the building with locked doors and found that this wasn't the right place. So we tried two more buildings before finding the right one.

Finally, I found the right man and was ushered into an impressive-looking room and told to sit down. He was grey-haired and was obviously an important man of the Iranian Oil Co. He explained that he was the only person who could contact Kharg Island because his line was direct to Abadan and then messages were radioed from Abadan to Kharg.

He was extremely pleased to let me phone, and it was wonderful talking to Claire, it was really great, to speak to someone I knew. Claire was thrilled to hear from me, but the line was not particularly good. Anyway, after chatting to her I asked the man how much I owed for the phone call, but he said it was free because it was not a telephone exchange, but a private company. This, I thought, was jolly good and kind. He was talking to me about the trip and said that if ever I went back to Tehran, for a holiday, or any other reason, I was to be sure to go to see him, but I can't remember his name. In the course of the conversation, I told him that dad used to work for Shell, and he said, "In that case, you deserve a free phone call."

Later I went on my own, in the dark, for two miles to collect my case from the coach, and although it was unnerving with men following and pushing, it wasn't as bad as Iraq, and as long as I ignored them completely, I was Ok

From Tehran, I wrote a letter home which said, "There is lots to do, and I don't like to miss anything, so I get tired by the end of the day. I suppose it's all the travelling and heat. You asked about hotel prices. Well, we have managed to get a room for as little as 3/- each, by five sharing a room for four. Who knows where you are when you're asleep, and saving money is our chief concern on this trip."

Day 39   1 November

TEHRAN TO ISFAHAN

Today we left Tehran at 7.30 a.m. and set off for
Isfahan, where we are to spend the night.

Well, I love the desert, it is so beautiful in Iran with
the wide valleys and high snow-capped mountains in
the distance. There are five days of desert travel left,
and the desert of Iraq was a bit bleak.

The journey today took us along a good, straight,
asphalt road, between craggy mountains on either side.
This broadened out into a flat, fertile valley with distant
hazy-blue mountains. We passed villages of domed
houses enclosed by walls. Most of the journey
continued through the arid desert and barren landscape.

On the way, we stopped for tea, and outside the chi
shop, several children stood watching us in amazement.

We are now in Isfahan and will be here for 4 nights
to explore one of Persia's most beautiful cities. We
arrived at Isfahan at about 3 p.m. and went to find a
hotel. We ended up with a plush hotel, with red
curtains, carpets and bedspreads, and hot showers for
10/- a night.

Today I was feeling ill, as there is a germ going
around which makes people sick, but it just succeeded
in making me feel jolly unhealthy. After settling into
the hotel, we went for a walk.

Isfahan is really great, with its cheerful shop lights,
and fairy light decorations for the Shah's birthday. Its
tree-lined main street was well set out and looked
attractive. It had cycle tracks so that cyclists were kept
separate from cars. In the centre of the dual
carriageway was a wide pavement for pedestrians. We
ate out and then went back to the hotel for coffee.

Day 40   2nd November

ISFAHAN TO PERSEPOLIS RETURN TO ISFAHAN

This morning most of us rose at 3 a.m. to leave at 4 a.m. for Persepolis. I do not regret today's outing at all. The journey was seven hours each way and we only stopped in Persepolis for two to three hours. Soon after dawn we passed a herd of goats, huddled together, being led by a goatherd.

The scenery was similar to yesterday, with mountains on either side of our valley. The sunrise was terrific, the best yet. A red glow spread across the sky and lightened into gold, all around, until the silhouetted mountains were clearly discernible. A few isolated villages were seen in the distance.

Persepolis consisted of majestic stone ruins of the Achaemenian capital, founded by Darius dating from 500 BC, and men were busy reconstructing them ready for next year when the Shah's anniversary will be celebrated there.

The gate of Xerxes stood in splendour, with two-headed monsters, on the ground, ready to be re-erected on top of the pillars.

The gate of the temple of a hundred pillars was decorated with ancient scenes of kings and armies, whilst other rocks bore similar carvings of people carrying gold.

Alexander the Macedonian destroyed Persepolis. The museum contained pottery and remains of the prehistoric, Islamic, and Hellenistic periods.

After here, we went to see the four tombs of Darius second, Darius the first, Xerxes, and Artaxerxes, which were all carved out of rock. At mid-day, it was extremely hot. My nylon trousers, that I was wearing clung to me uncomfortably. During the ride back to Isfahan, we saw the sunset and stars appear in its place. Then the lights of Isfahan were most welcomingly sighted in the distance, twinkling, and sparkling

Day 41   3rd November

ISFAHAN

At 9 a.m. we went on a conducted coach tour of Isfahan. The Blue Mosques were absolutely beautiful with their azure-blue tiles and mosaics. Never before have I seen such man-made splendour. They looked beautiful with the sun shining on them, making them glint and flash sparkles of light. The Shah Mosque is a UNESCO World Heritage site now. Its construction began in 1611. It has a beautiful, blue-tiled mosaic dome and an interesting three-dimensional honeycomb effect structure on the porch roof.

We visited old mosques and new, and one with shaking minarets, where a man went up into the minaret and swayed against the walls so that it shook. It looked dangerous, but it has lasted 700 years and is still there. The Masjed-e-Jame is also known as the Friday Mosque. It is the oldest mosque in Isfahan spanning twelve centuries from AD 841, so is a stunning illustration of the evolution of mosque architecture and art. It is also one of the UNESCO World Heritage sites now. There are ten in Isfahan today.

Nearby, about three miles from Isfahan was a Zoroastrian Fire Temple. This is the oldest ruin of anything to be found, in or around Isfahan, and dates back to 700 BC. Fire, which produces white ash, and water were used as purification agents in their ceremonies, believing that they would receive happiness. "Whoever sacrifices unto fire with fuel in his hand ..., is given happiness". Zoroastrianism is an ancient Iranian religion.

We visited an art museum of miniatures, which were superbly made, and so clever. I have never been interested in such art, but after seeing these I was really intrigued and liked them. Next, we visited a Persian carpet factory, where women sat patiently making carpets. It takes three women one year to make a carpet two by three metres. Each woman sits at a loom with all the coloured balls of wool strung across in a line in front of her. She has a small picture of the rug, and a large picture of the piece she is making.

We viewed an unusual bridge, with a double layer of arches, one above the other, and an upstairs pathway called the Khaja Bridge. This bridge can control the flow of water through the use of sluices, damming the river if needed.

In my letter home, I wrote, "Isfahan is the best place on route yet, with its blue mosques, minarets, and blue tiles. Now we are off to see the bazaar where they beat copper and silver, and I hope I don't spend too much money."

In the afternoon we went to the covered Grand Bazaar, part of which was built in the eleventh century and the remainder over the centuries, particularly the seventeenth. It is very big and easy to get lost. The ceilings are high and lofty, so the passageways are airy and noisy. The market is divided into sections, so that similar things are all in the same area, such as spices, material, jewellery, food, handicrafts, inlaid, and others.

We walked around the smells of spices, food, and soaps, and saw such beautiful, coloured material. This section of the market is called the Mesgarha, which means the coppersmith's Alley. Some of these workshops were also outside. I saw the copper sheets cut into shape and fired, then hammered and smoothed for sale.

Inside we came across silver and copper beaters industriously hammering out articles to sell, pots, pans, trays, jugs, jewellery. It was very noisy. The banging echoed all around. Even after all these years, I can still remember that sound.

Carpets and rugs, known as Killim, are a speciality. We saw the entire process taking place. A man invited us to go through a dark doorway to see a camel walking round and round, grinding seed for the dyes. The poor old camel just kept trudging round, and its eyes were blindfolded. Further through was another camel. Then we were taken up onto the roof where skeins of dyed, coloured wool hung out in the sunshine to dry. These would make carpets. Some carpets are made of wool, others silk and some silk and wool.

We visited a miniatures shop, above a shop in the market, where miniature pictures were made. This was fascinating to watch. I bought one. It was a small picture from an historic event, painted on bone, and framed in an inlaid frame. Next door we watched hand-printing done on material.

Isfahan was memorable. It seemed such an industrious, well-set-out, clean place. There was a real difference between these people, who are industrious and conscientious workers, and those of Jordan and Iraq. It was so refreshing to see craftsmen working hard, after several weeks of idle, bottom-pinching men. I lost the others here and had to find my own way back through the market and crowds to the hotel.

Tonight, nineteen of us went to a party held at the house of an English nurse. The party was given by eight people from the European Workers Association. There were forty in Iran and eight in Isfahan. It was similar to

Voluntary Service Overseas and International Voluntary Service, and they nurse in ordinary and mental homes. The team consists of English, Dutch, and Norwegians. At the party, there were also German and American Peace Corps workers. They are a similar organization doing engineering, architecture, and teaching. Some other people there were from Yorkshire. They were supervising a woollen factory outside Isfahan.

We stood around chatting, drinking, and talking. Tables and chairs were set in the garden, with candles around the pond, but it was so very cold out there that oil heaters had to be taken out. Inside the house, there was no furniture visible, and everyone had to stand amid soft lights and music. The weather was cold and stone floors didn't help.

Day 42   4th November

ISFAHAN

Isfahan has attracted visitors for over 300 years. It was in the early 17th century, under Shah Abbas, that the city became known as Isfahan-Nesf-e-Jahan, which means Isfahan is half the world. In those days Muslims, Christians, Jews, and Armenians mingled in its streets. British and Dutch merchants haggled in its bazaars over the prices of Isfahan carpets, spices from India, or the merchandise brought by camel caravan from Samarkand and Bokhara. Swiss watchmakers, Chinese potters, and Persian silversmiths worked day and night pouring out a stream of prized craftsmanship, for which the city is still famous.

This morning it was wonderful to be able to laze about and get up when we wished. At 10 a.m. I went down to the market to take photographs, but as it was mosque day and their weekend, there was not much activity going on; but it was interesting to see the craftsmen working without fighting through crowds of shoppers. Children went out of their way to speak, and one even offered me a ride in his little box on wheels!

The afternoon was spent chatting, writing, and then shopping. We had to buy some emergency rations for the desert, as five days of desert lay ahead. I did buy some silver jewellery for myself; it was not expensive but a nice reminder and was handcrafted. I also bought a small doll dressed in a local costume, for my growing collection.

This trip is so exciting and fantastically thrilling. On one side is an air of expectancy, on the other is a glowing remembrance of experiences, whilst the present is full of interest and wonder.

WEEK SEVEN

Day 43   5th November

ISFAHAN TO YAZD

The journey today took us from Isfahan to Yazd. Leaving Isfahan at 7 am we went on **the Great Asian Highway** across the arid desert. Unfortunately, the tarmacadam section of this road finishes about two hours' motor drive out of Isfahan and the rest of the trip was on dust road and will be for the remainder of our journey. Eventually, it is hoped that the Asian highway will be right across to India, Malaya, and Singapore, but this will take some while to complete.

The weather was very cool, and jumpers and coats were required for warmth, although it was up over 60F degrees. Sun was shining, and the desert mountains seemed to emerge from a mist of sand and looked grand on either side of the wide valley.

On the way, we saw many humps in lines, and these were covered wells. When they were made, a small boy went down the hole with a candle, and a piece of string, and dug along until the candle went out, because the oxygen was used up. The length of the tunnel was then measured with string, across the surface from that hole, and another hole was dug. So oxygen circulated. We saw one of these wells being cleaned out by means of a wooden wheel, which was man manipulated, and a leather bucket put down on a rope, and the mud lifted out and tipped out to one side.

I noticed a man making bricks. He mixed mud and straw together with a spade. The houses and walls were made of straw, mud, and camel dung, and blended into the surrounding scenery beautifully. The houses have domed roofs and looked picturesque. When we arrived at **Yazd,** a camel train was walking across the road. Each camel was tied to the one before and behind it.

Yazd has a clock tower; of which it is proud because not many places in Persia possess these.

Yazd is the centre of Zoroastrianism, one of the world's most ancient religions. With only a few thousand followers left, these devotees of Darkness and Light worship in their Fire Temples and still expose their dead in huge Towers of Silence, which are seen on the surrounding hills.

We stayed at the Guest House, the cost of putting a camp bed up in a large communal room was 1/-.

Parched with thirst I eagerly opened my tin of fruit, which was to be my main meal of the day. Imagine my dismay, when the juice shot up to the ceiling, the whole lot was bad, so I had to go to sleep and forget my stomach.

Day 44   6th   November

YAZD TO BAM

We woke up at 4 a.m., ready to leave at 5 a.m. to avoid the heat of the day, also the hour before dawn is the coldest in the desert, and at that time we were moving about, instead of getting cold in bed. This morning's sunrise was the best yet, not a cloud in sight, just a red glowing sky with mountains silhouetted against it.

The road, of course, was very dusty, and no sooner had we begun than we were clouded out with sand particles inside the coach, it was alarming. Dust sucks up through vents in the floor and through removable flooring. Everything got covered, as per yesterday, and after an hour or so my hair was grey, and all our clothes, cameras, bags, and cases were coated in this fine, suffocating sand.

Quickly people put on their yashmaks, scarves, or handkerchiefs. One New Zealand man, aged about the early 60s, had a smog mask. He looked so funny sitting there, and even funnier when he got out and strolled along the desert looking like a native in unusual costume, with trousers tucked into his socks, sun hat on, and head held erectly in the air, with a muzzle attached. It looked comical to see him strutting, unassumingly, rather like a chicken.

The scenery was the same as yesterday, but I love it so much. We travel for two or three hundred miles and every time we look out of the window the scenery is exactly the same. It is as if we are travelling along a wide valley with rugged mountains on either side, and I am so curious to know just what lies over the other side. I wonder if it is more mountains or desert.

Every couple of hours we stopped at a chi shop for tea. These little buildings are set in the midst of nowhere and are like transport cafes, and as soon as anyone arrives, the man quickly gets his urn boiling, or if we arrive too early, he has to open up and start the fire burning. Inside there are no seats, but carpeted flooring, also people sit on large windowsills, or raised partitions, like huge steps, with Persian carpets covering them. Tea costs as little as one penny, in old English money, and is not too bad, if you are thirsty and like tea.

At 1.30 p.m. we arrived at **Kerman,** a desert town. This place really impressed me, for it is the first place we've been to that doesn't cater specifically for tourists but is really authentic. Women washed clothes in the streets, where water flowed down the gutters, and people seemed so friendly. They chatted to us and smiled, and they were very good-looking people.

The place seemed clean, and we went for a walk through the bazaar, which, to me, was the best yet, clean and tidy, and people willing to help. In fact, we got a train of followers that followed us through the market and found us entertaining, particularly when we took photos.

Walking through the narrow back alleys between the houses was an experience. There were many arches and arched supports crossing the alleys. One or two of the women were scared of us, which surely indicated that this is not a "tourist resort."

Overall, there was something warm and welcoming about this place and I liked it. It must have been the friendly people. Some poor, distorted beggars sat about the market, and women squatted in corners, with babies. I noticed other women squatting together in the streets chatting, instead of standing on street corners like they do at home.

Two or three men were selling Persian carpets in Kerman. They lay them down on the cobbled stone street for inspection. I thought it was a shame to put such magnificent handiwork onto a dusty place. Kerman is renowned as the chief centre for the best Persian carpets. This fact was noted by Marco Polo as he went through there in the thirteenth century.

To me, the desert holds a fascination, a warm mystery. I love the feel of sun-baked sand slipping between my toes, and I love the loneliness. There is peace in the desert and a feeling of space, yet beauty, with a backdrop of beautiful mountains.

The guest house we stayed at was a typical sort, with a pond and courtyard, and rooms all around in a square. Tonight was particularly thrilling, for we met up with the other Penn Bus, which is going in the opposite direction. They have had trouble with the bus, and India and Pakistan border, and are now eleven days behind schedule, which makes us realise what an easy time we are having in comparison. There were also eight of the American Peace corps. at this place, and Dot and I had a most enjoyable time talking to one of the fellows. Got to bed at 11.30 p.m.

Day 45   7th November

BAM TO ZAHEDAN

Up just after 4 a.m. and left about 5.15 a.m. At first, the scenery was much the same as before, but it wasn't so dusty, so perhaps a bit stonier.

On the way, we passed snow-capped mountains, and when we stopped, ice lay on the water, and icicles hung from a water tap. This, in the middle of the Iranian desert, so it just shows how cold it can be at night. These days across the desert have been very cold.

This morning, just after the sun had risen, we stopped at Mahan, at a beautiful mosque, with well-kept gardens, with ponds.

Through the gardens and arches, we came to the mosque which is a memorial to Shah Nematollah Vali, who was a 15th-century poet and mystic, and Sufi leader, who died in 1431.

It was a bit creepy inside, with candles burning around a tomb. When we came out, we found that men had turned all our shoes round, ready to step into, kind of them. The outside of the mosque was blue-tiled, but the inside was very plain.

We had a chi stop for three-quarters of an hour, and Frank mended the radiator. At this stop were three G.B. cars.

It is great fun on this trip because we are always coming across lots of other people doing the same thing, in buses, cars, and jeeps, and it's jolly interesting hearing of their future plans. One car was full of a Pakistani family who had just come from Manchester, and it had only taken them two weeks to do it, as opposed to our six weeks.

Later, the scenery became more desert-looking, with a vast expanse of sand and no mountains. Lunch stop, for three-quarters of an hour, was taken at a beautiful spot, where there were large rocks, and desert plants grew in profusion, and trees swayed and rustled in the strengthening wind.

Between the date-growing oasis of Bam and Zahedan, lies the southern fringe of the Dasht-i-lut desert. The road across is about 30 miles long and is marked by old desert lighthouses.

The lighthouses guided the travellers safely through the shifting sands. Caravans often travelled at night, so the tops of these towers were lit with flares, and during the day, gave off smoke. This was many years before the era of combustion engines,

We came to a desert lighthouse and went in. Although the spiral steps were dangerous, I just had to go up for the sheer fun of it, but after clambering and stumbling up in my old wooden sandals, which were not the best shoes to go in, I got the biggest shock of my life, when I suddenly ran out of walls and found myself on the top step, which was the roof!

The wind was blowing hard, and I looked down and saw the coach and lots of people, like specks on the desert road. I sat down quickly before I fell over the top because I can't stand heights. Luckily, Barry was there to act the gentleman, and he took my hand as we went back down the stairs, but I'm glad I went up. In this desert, we wore scarves that we drew over our faces when sand was blowing.

We were in the Dasht-E-Lut, the second great desert of central Iran. Soon over this barren stretch of sand, with shimmering mirages in abundance, looking like ponds and lakes, one could even see trees and large birds or animals by the water, but they all disappeared into thin air as we approached.

We began a steep climb over a mountain pass and down to **Zahedan,** arriving at 5.30 p.m. The mountains were colourful and beautifully folded and stratified, until the sun's last rays shone leaving them just a silhouette.

Hotel price 4/- bed and 4/- evening meal. Tonight people were wandering up the street playing one or two instruments. I think they were a one-stringed fiddle.

Day 46   8ᵗʰ November

ZAHEDAN TO DALBANDIN

We left fairly early again because time would be spent in crossing the border into Pakistan. The ride to the Iran border was not too long, but once again we saw the sunrise. This is becoming quite a common occurrence.

We arrived at the Iran border at about 7.30 a.m. and had time to wander around this little village, while we waited for official business. We were quite taken by the national costumes, but unfortunately, the people wouldn't allow us to take photographs, or rather the police wouldn't. This happens at every border, no photos.

Eighty miles further on we came to the **Pakistan border.** It was terribly hot here, and crowds and crowds of children gathered round to look at us, to point and shout, and generally get in the way.

It was also lunchtime, but there were so many flies, that it was impossible to eat outside without getting the food covered with them. At **Nok Kunde,** the border town, water had to be transported by train, so trains stood beside the customs hut, and water was rationed, and sold. After a couple of hours, we were allowed through.

Pakistan is very British, and remnants of signs are billeted at various points along the road, even in the desert. We laughed about the abundance of signs because they were so stupid, either they indicated a bend in the straight desert road, or else suddenly put a bend sign which made us wonder just which bend they meant.

We are now in **Baluchistan,** the bare land of nomadic tribes, whose life is spent in seasonal migrations to new pastures. Soon we were in **Dalbandin,** a little sandy village where there was a hospital for sick camels.

We stayed in a rest house and camped out in a jungle garden, with our beds set on the veranda. The moon was shining, crickets chirping, dogs barking and howling in the distance. Palm trees and tropical shrubs surrounded a pond full of goldfish.

In this setting, around a bright hurricane lamp, a group of white-robed, turbaned men, sat cross-legged, seriously discussing, and writing, several other men stood watching, hovering amongst the shrubs.

It was dark, so creepy walking in the grounds. Suddenly, there would be a rustle amongst the leaves, and when a torch was shone in the direction of the noise, it would shine on a man just following or watching us. This gathering of official men turned out to be a local court being held.

There were no toilet facilities at all, so we all had to "go bush," upon the sand dunes, behind the guest house. This was difficult, to say the least by torchlight, and I managed to lose my shoe in the soft sand, and we had to go digging for it.

Supper was served in our own dishes, and we sat eating outside, while scruffy old men and dogs stood watching, waiting for scraps. We threw the bones to dogs, who pounced and tore them apart with relish, but as soon as anyone went to throw the scraps, a little man insisted that we put them in his bowl. We thought that this was so that he could give them to the dogs tidily, but to our horror, he went around the side of the building and ate them himself.

It was too awful for words to see these poor old chaps watching us eat, hoping that we wouldn't eat it all, but save some for them. I didn't realise this until I had almost finished mine, but the thought of it made the remainder of the food just stick in my throat.

There was running water laid on for us especially. This was a pipe that filled the goldfish pond. As we washed here, a man kept appearing and telling us not to put soap in the pond in case it killed the fish. I think the dirt alone would have done this.

Once we were washing, and I was aware of someone watching, so shining the torch up amongst the bushes, at my side, I saw a lad crouching and watching in silence. One man followed Liz and me when we went across to see Barry, who was ill and staying in a hut, and when we stopped, he stopped. Then when Liz spoke to him, he just stood like a statute. It was fearful, we expected him to draw out a knife at any time and thrust it through us.

This place really impressed me and reminded me of the films I've seen of white people living in stately homes in jungle areas when they are being hunted out by people, and as they walk into the gardens at night, so faces keep appearing, and animals howl and snakes slither up. It was just the same idea here.

Day 47   9th November

DALBANDIN TO QUETTA

We had breakfast at 4.30 a.m. and left before dawn, so once more watched the sunrise. We travelled through part of Baluchistan, in northern Pakistan, through an arid desert area, and skirted the granite Chagai Hills. On the way, we passed a signpost to London, 5,686 miles, where a man was posing beside it with his tinsel-trimmed bike.

A little further along we met some of the Baluchi tribe. They were trailing along in a line on the move from their summer homes, in the mountains, to their winter homes on the plains. They had children and goats, camels, and donkeys with chickens, and a very few other items, tied on top. People in the countries we have passed through, often tie chickens' legs together, and tuck the creatures under their arms, like this they can clamber onto buses, or just sit on the pavement with them. These people tied chickens on top of donkeys, I had never seen that before. They had everything they needed. Chickens for eggs, goats for milk, camels and donkeys for transport and work.

Today's ride took us through the mountainous area. and over the steep gradient of **Lak Pass to Quetta.**
We arrived in Quetta at about 2 p.m. The hotel people were outside to meet us, but we were going to drive around Quetta before going to the hotel, so every time we passed the end of the hotel, someone shot out after us, it was quite funny.

We called at the Afghan Embassy, and they gave permission for us to get visas that day. There was great rejoicing all round. At first we thought our bus would be too long to managed the narrow, winding roads, but we learned, from other travellers at Kerman that we could manage the Khyber Pass alright. I was thrilled.

We stayed in Quetta for two days. The hotel was fabulous, after what we have had, it was like flats. We had suits for two, consisting of lounge, bedroom, and bathroom, with HOT water. Such a welcome change.

I opened my case after the hotel chap had dusted off half an inch of desert dust, and inside everything was coated with sand. So out came the lot, and I made full use of the hot water washing everything.

We had afternoon tea at 4 pm and then dinner at 7.30 p.m. The food here was good. As Barry was ill, I did his washing. We didn't go out tonight, but Margaret and I went into Gill and Jeans for coffee and biscuits, and I took my tape recorder, and played music, for entertainment and we had a very enjoyable evening.

The night was cold, so coal and wood were provided for the fire.

Day 48   10th November

QUETTA

Quetta, the old British hill station that once guarded the passes of the Northwest Frontier, is situated high up in the mountains.

Today was free to explore. We walked into town. I didn't expect it to be very interesting, but it was full of fascinating things. Its bazaar was full of industrious sellers. It was a large open market of streets and streets of shops. Each area sold different goods, such as a jewellery section and food section, and so on.

We went to various banks in order to change a traveller's cheque of mine into sterling. At last, we found one, but they took my passport and requested me to return at 3 p.m. when they would be able to say if permission had been granted. They did get Stirling for me but endorsed my passport greatly and were under the impression that I would be returning to the UK after India.

The funniest things are the taxis, which I just had to try. So, after dinner, we went into town by a local taxi. They are gaily decorated, little three-wheeled things, with two-stroke engines, like a miniature milk float, with accommodation for two people in the back. They are covered in bits of tinsel, coloured plastic draping's, cords, chains, coins dangling from them, and anything bright stuck on them.

They charged full pelt up the road at 20 m.p.h. Rocked over ruts, as they swerved around horses and carts. Jumped in the air, as they hurtled over bumps and lumps in the road, and swerved around cars, horses, and carts. Death-traps. Well, a ride in one of these was an experience worth having but was a bit like riding on a switch-back at the fair. It was like a ride to death. Flashing up the road in one of these, we had to hang on for dear life and hoped and prayed we would get there. We walked back.

Women of the Balochi tribe sat in the street making embroidered articles, and several shops sold these goods. As they were only peculiar to this district, I just had to buy a piece of dress material. Mirrors are sewn into their work, and each is secured by sixty to seventy stitches.

We gazed into one window, in the material market and were invited in to see a couple of chaps embroidering velvet. It was lovely work. The material was in a frame, and silver thread was sewn into place, and secured with cotton. Threaded beads were also worked into the pattern.

After supper, we lit our fire and sat there in comfort, Gill and Jean had come in, and shortly a couple of girls called from the International Voluntary Service, who we had met earlier. A Pakistan fellow brought them, and we were all invited to their friend's house. This was above a photographer's shop, owned by the fellow. Kept warm by electric fires, we sat chatting.

The girls were at a mission hospital, and one of the boys lived in the compound, as his mother was matron there. He told us that many relatives arrived with the patients at the hospital and moved in with their animals. They came to look after the patient and feed her. Maureen was one of these girls and she was small in stature but had a confident, reassuring voice, the sort that held you captive as soon as she spoke. She obviously was a suitable person to be sent to work amongst these people.

Elizabeth, the other girl, had been in Quetta eighteen months and had six months to go. She had often been sent to nurse tribe's people, away from the hospital. Actually, it sounded interesting for them to travel around and learn so much. There are several languages, but apparently "boys" at the hospital can interpret for the nurses. We were taken back again by car, at 1 a.m., after an interesting evening.

My letter home said, "Isn't it terrific, tomorrow we are going to Afghanistan! The route has been changed to go here instead of across more deserts, to make it more interesting. I am so thrilled because now we will go through the Khyber Pass, and to Kandahar and Kabul.

I am simply loving this journey, and enthusiasm has increased as we came across the desert and left Arab land behind. What a difference between the Iraqis, Pakistanis, and Iranians. The people of Pakistan are lovely. They are good-looking, polite, and don't bother us as we walk down the road.

The desert is a wonderful place, I love it, with its vast expanse of sand and mountains beyond, and the sunrises and sunsets are better than I've ever seen before. Yes, I've seen sunrises. We have been getting up at 4 a.m. to leave at 5 a.m. We are now five hours ahead of you in time, so when you are having tea, I'm going to bed. The sunsets of the desert glow red and a mauve colour that we never see at home. There is a feeling of space in the desert, and all day long we don't pass more than twelve to twenty people.

It's a laugh when we arrive at our destination each day because crowds of people gather around the bus to see us, and just stare in wonderment, often the police have to come and move them off. This letter must be written in haste, as now it is the next day and the bus will soon be leaving, we hope. It is due to go at 11 a.m. because it had to have a spare part found.

I am looking forward to what is to come in and beyond this trip, on the one hand, and on the other, I am looking back with happy memories of what we have seen. Looking back paints a better picture of Arab land than actually being there, because I tend to forget the discomfort and bad parts, and only remember the good.

Travelling with dysentery, with sweat pouring off, through boiling hot weather well above 100 degrees isn't very funny; and then getting up at 4 a.m. and not arriving at the destination until after dark, sometimes very tired and feeling unhealthy, not able to eat and too tired to do anything but put up a camp bed and get into a sleeping bag, at times, made me think "Why ever did I come?" but I only thought it occasionally. I don't regret giving up my job to come, in fact, I don't feel as if I can ever be bothered with a career again! I will be an odd job lay about, or if you can find a suitable person Dad you might be able to sell me when I come back!!

Now it is cold and there's a nip in the air, and in two weeks' time there should be snow on the ground about two feet deep, and it will be colder in Afghanistan, but their furs and leather are cheap so I might stock up.

Food is a terrific price here. Cheese of six portions costs 9/-, and a tin of meat about the same, so you can guess I'm not going to bother much with it.

I expect, now in November, you are sitting by a nice warm coal fire in the dining room, with mist outside, or some fog. How lovely and cosy it must be, not having to bother what time you get up in the mornings, and then people calling in the day and at evening, and you can sit and chat and have cups of tea. It's lovely to think of, and is such a good, contented existence.

Please tell me all the news about everyone, and who has been, and who hasn't. My mind constantly turns to home. I'm not homesick, because I wouldn't have missed this trip for anything. But home is where the heart is, and that is what I am looking forward to. To have achieved my ambition and come back home.

I can't wait to see Beryl in Australia, and won't it be lovely to go to New Zealand with her, far more fun than going alone.

Please will you tell everyone who has written to me that I shall write after the bus trip when I get time, because I even find it such a tight schedule that I only squeeze your letters in with effort and my diary is over a week behind, there's so much to see and do, and everything is so strange and fascinating and new, that I don't like to miss anything.

I am spending on average £1 per day, and that is going very carefully. It breaks my heart to see the others, on their way home, of course, spending lots of money on lovely things that I would love, and I just keep remembering your words mum, "There's a big difference between what you want and what you need," and that keeps my purse strings tied.

You know, I will never alter, I find it terribly hard to be selfish on this trip. Most people are very independent and think of themselves, and I am gradually learning to be a bit like it, because you have to be, to survive. In fact, in the hot climate I only had sufficient energy and strength each day to keep my mind on my own needs and activities, but now, I have drifted back to my usual self, and yesterday Barry was ill and so I did his washing.

I like looking after people and that's what I miss now I'm away from home. I don't expect people to think any the better of anybody for helping them, but that is not the purpose, **I believe that as a Christian I should show love towards others, and not be selfish, and not do things for what one gets in return.**

My feet are so split because of the dry sand, that even the chemists were horrified, now I must keep my feet covered and bandaged. God bless you and I know He will look after you, so I've nothing to worry about. Love from Elizabeth

Day 49   11th November

QUETTA TO KANDAHAR AFGHANISTAN

This morning the bus was not due to leave until 11 a.m., in order to get a spare part, but in actual fact, we didn't leave until almost 1 p.m.

Margaret and I wanted to buy some bread from a shop we had previously been to, in the market. Taking a paper bag with us, showing the address of this shop, we went across the road and got a horse-drawn taxicab. This is a horse and trap. These little cabs accommodate two passengers, who ride back-to-back with the driver.

When I went to get in the thing I felt as if it was going to tip up. To get in you had to stand on a small step, and immediately any pressure was put on this, the whole cab rocked backwards. Once seated inside, or half outside, for there was just a canopy for protection, we set off down the road. The driver busily whips the horse to make it go faster.

Some carts are decorated with bits of tinsel, and bells that dangle and jangle as the cart goes up the road. The bells sound pretty, harmonising with the horses' hoofs on stone. It was a rough ride, as we went over hollows, bumps, and dents in the road, and although our driver tried to make the horse trot faster, by giving an occasional whip, it made absolutely no difference, for our poor old horse just went its own sweet way, and kept up a steady pace of about 15 m.p.h.

At the market, there were crowds of men, but very few women. Our purchasing complete, and a visit to the Post Office, we went back to the hotel by one of the motor taxis.

As soon as we started to load everything into the bus, crowds, and crowds of people crowded around, watching us with fixed attention. It seemed as if half the population had come to see us off. Oxen trudged along, heaving carts behind them. Camels pranced by, kicking out their legs in a cheeky fashion. Heads were thrown back with pride, as they pulled carts of bricks. Bells on their knees and round their necks jingled merrily.

The route out to the **Afghanistan border** took us up over the **Chaman Pass to Chaman the border town.** What a pass!! It was a dust road, carved out of the mountainside, and wound and bent this way and that. If I hadn't had confidence in the driver, I wouldn't have felt at all at ease, for the road was narrow and twisty with quite a drop on one side.

When we reached the top of the pass, there was a board stating that we were over 7,500 feet above sea level. The view down, over the mountains, and ribbon road, winding through them, to the plain beyond, was beautiful. If there hadn't been mistiness about it would have been even better.

At the Pakistan border with Afghanistan, we all got out to have our picnic lunch, and the population just swarmed on us. It was not only the children who came, but fathers brought their toddlers, and grandfathers came too. Not content with just watching us, they clambered around and asked for whisky and baksheesh.

As the crowd thickened, several people decided that it was time to settle down, in a squatting position, in the front row to get an unobstructed view of the foreigners eating. We had two boiled eggs and bread, and it wasn't particularly appetizing to start with, but when they started sniffing, spluttering, coughing, and spitting about the place, as we ate, it was difficult to eat.

In the end one of them picked up a large stone to throw at us, then others and children, copied, and when we ducked there were shrieks of laughter. These people were certainly not the type to upset, they seemed crude, hard, and vicious. Frank went to the bus and sounded the horn indicating for us to get on. We were relieved and quickly went on our way. Afghanistan's seemed severe, and we were warned not to laugh at them. We crossed the border into Afghanistan and soldiers with guns stared at us, as much as the other locals had.

After a while, the customs officer told us all to get back into our "machine," and we were off. Clocks were put back half an hour, which made us four and a half hours ahead of England.

The drive to **Kandahar** took just over one hour on the straight road. Lorries did not have reflectors, which made it dangerous when passing parked vehicles in the dark. The hotel at Kandahar was built of stone and was large, and roomy. Inside it was cold and spacious. Lots of us put up camp beds in bedrooms for the sake of economy, and seven shared our bedroom designed for three, which brought the cost down to about 3/9 each. Dinner was tasty, but sparse, and consisted of rice, baked potatoes, and meat, and cost 3/9. Tea was served in the lounge.

There was a real character in the party, she was Anastasia Romanoff. She turned out to be quite a loner, and I remember by the time we reached Afghanistan no one could persuade her to leave the coach at night, and she refused to eat anything, other than oranges. I felt sorry for her and would often walk about with her listening to her stories, until, one day, Roger, the courier warned me, "Take care that a person does not sap your energy on a journey like this, for this is no ordinary expedition." He was right to a certain extent.

WEEK EIGHT

Day 50   12th November

KANDAHAR TO KABUL

This morning we stopped, for half an hour, in **Kandahar** market, which was unique, it was situated in a long street. The road was a dust road and open shops lined each side. Men sold different wares, but particularly curved knives. It was unnerving and suggested an atmosphere of impending danger. I didn't feel at ease in Afghanistan, seeing guns and knives sold.

Women were mostly kept out of sight, and children seemed to be looked after by the men. I saw meat hanging outside the butcher's shop, and people were handling and feeling it before they bought it.

Women wore veils of assorted colours, finely pleated, from the headpiece downwards, hiding their eyes. One of the International Voluntary Service girls in Quetta told us that women's eyesight in Afghanistan were affected by wearing thick face coverings, which did not let in much light. Being in purdah made them get poor vision.

They also said that one missionary doctor has been allowed into Afghanistan, provided that he doesn't preach, and if any in the country becomes Christians from Muslims, they will be killed.

We stopped at a chi shop for tea. A man sat smoking a Hubble bubble pipe, then lifted the corner of the mat and spat under it!! Dorothy, Malcolm, Barry, Martin, Susanne, Liz, and I sat outside on the ground where an Afghan man joined us, and we all had our photos taken.

The long journey was beautiful with grand, lofty mountains that could be seen clearly on this crisp, sunny day. The lunch stop was a picnic stop in a little mud hut village, and as we sat eating, so a man kept guard with his gun. Then another old man came along, took off his shoes, and bowed in the direction of Mecca, as it was prayer time.

We arrived in **Kabul** in time to go back into town for supper, at a good western-style restaurant. Here, again, fires were lit in our rooms, these were boilers which really warmed the place.

I shared a bed with Annett, equal and plus, in size to me, but it wasn't a good idea at all in such a small space, because I ran out of covers. Here it was not the beds, but the rooms that were let, so we could get more people in using camp beds and sleeping bags, which made it economical.

Day 51   13th November

KABUL

The morning was spent trying to change money at the bank, but service was so slow that when we came out it was lunchtime. After lunch, we visited the scruffiest, dirtiest market I have ever seen anywhere.

Anyway, we picked our way over mud and slime, and open sewerage, past hovels of houses with cracked mud peeling off the walls. Just below, stalls were erected. These were selling jewellery, and shoes with turned-up toes like pixies shoes. The maker couldn't understand why we didn't want to buy any.

Then on to places where old pieces of metal from cars were being beaten and made into other articles for sale. This struck me as being very resourceful. There didn't appear to be as many beggars as we had seen in other countries, and I wondered if, perhaps, the people were a bit more industrious.

One shack in the market was crammed full of children. This must have been their school, and as we stood watching, so they lifted their books and read as loud as they could, all saying something different. It was obviously done to impress us. Later we discovered shops selling leather coats, and I bought a sheepskin, embroidered jacket for £3, it was such a bargain that I couldn't miss it.

Kabul wasn't as I expected it to be, it was far dirtier and scruffier, and not nearly so clean and beautiful, as I had imagined. It was straggling and lay on either side of a river.

Water isn't good to drink here, because it runs parallel to the sewerage, and gets contaminated, and it isn't even safe for cleaning teeth. I found out all this after I had drunk it. I had taken a supply of water sterilising tablets with me, and one of the girls used a bit of bleach. Not recommended. 2% of the population are literate, so not much wonder drainage and water are not good.

Day 52   14th November

KABUL TO ISLAMABAD

The drive today took us past cattle and camel markets with tents everywhere. The journey led out through the **Kabul Gorge**. This is the most wonderful mountain pass I have ever seen in all my life. The mountains just towered up, to lofty heights, and left me quite breathless in wonder. Quickly we drew the roof curtains back so that the peaks of the mountains could be observed.

The road hugged the foot of the mountain and wound on and on until we came to the Afghan border. This was a large white building, set amidst a garden full of trees. Here we ate lunch, and in about half an hour were through customs, and off again.

More time was spent at the Pakistan frontier, and men sat about performing their favourite habit of this region, of clearing their throats and spitting. I'm sure they try to see who can spit the furthest. A revolting habit.

Soon we were winding our way up over the **Khyber Pass.** This was quite attractive, but nothing at all in comparison to the wonderful Kabul Gorge. At the top, we stopped to take pictures and saw a signpost marking one route for cars, and another for camel traffic. The descent over the mountains brought us into **Islamabad,** around 9.30 p.m. There was only one hotel available, and this was absolute luxury. The long driveway was marked with a line of tiny oil lamps and loads of servants stood around waiting to serve. The other hotels in Rawalpindi were all occupied by the banker's conference, so we had to take this place.

One room, for two, cost £5, so we were given permission to camp. We had five in our room and so the price between us was good. There were showers, and although only lukewarm, were valuable to us. We just have to hear the word shower now, and jump at a place, irrespective of price.

Day 53   15th November

ISLAMABAD TO LAHORE

Breakfast was superb, and eggs were served one of six ways. It was a slap-up meal, with excellent service, with music floating softly through the air, English music at that.

First, we called at the Embassy for permission to take our non-commonwealth passengers through the Pakistan, Indian border, but on being told that we had to get it at Lahore we continued our journey to **Lahore.**

All the time ox carts and cattle got in the way, so we shot up the road, blasting the horn furiously, to shift them.

It was not as bad as last night, where we couldn't see the animals because they had no lights, and when it was like an obstacle race, also last night we had to cross a bridge and had a very tricky manoeuvring session to get on, while we held up a train of camels. We slowly crossed a narrow wooden pontoon bridge at Lahore, following an ox cart. The width of our bus just fitted.

Lahore looked like an overpopulated, dirty, dilapidated old place. People swarmed around us every time we stopped, and buildings were chipped, plaster falling off and windows were broken, or out. In fact, we wondered what place we had been led to.

This was the old part and we stayed in the Young Women's Christian Association in the new part. The full board was 6/-.

Here we met Vanessa, and Sue and I shared her room, on camp beds. She had been here 8 nights waiting for us.

The warden was a dominant, plump Pakistani, who kept law and order pleasantly. At this place, my food bag was running alive with ants.

Some of the others stayed at a post hotel for £2 a day, but 1/- a night was more my mark. Today we crossed the **Indus tributaries**.

Day 54   16th November

LAHORE

Sue and I went by scooter taxi to see some of the places of interest in Lahore. First of all, we went to the Badshah Mosque, which is the largest mosque in the world. It was built in the 1670s.

We had to take our shoes off, as we do in all mosques, but as well as this, the man took one look at our legs and issued us with old draping to cover them up. We laughed, and so did the locals because we looked just like old washerwomen, or grannies in long skirts. Somehow, even with these hindering our stride, we still managed to climb to the top of a high minaret, where we had a beautiful view across Lahore.

Just outside the grounds of the mosque, we saw a white building, known as the Samadhi, which contains the cremated remains of Ranjit Singh,1780-1839. He was the first Maharaja of the Sikh Empire and was known as the Lion of the Punjab.

From here, we went across to the Fort, which was right next to the Badshah mosque. A man tried his utmost to be a guide, but, because of our money situation, we declined his offer.

At the fort we met Stephanie and John, and wandered around the old place together, looking at bullet marks and admiring flower gardens, and a lovely pond. While we were there, a party from the Bankers Conference arrived, proudly striding around. We saw a man walking along with a snake around his arm.

We hired a buggy cart to take us to the Shalimar Gardens. First bargaining to fix a price before departing, and the poor old mare took about one and a half hours to get us there. He plodded along, quite wearily, and all the other buggies passed us by.

The Gardens were superb. Entering under a large arch, we were spellbound, at the absolute beauty. In front of us was a long lake, flanked either side by gardens, and further up was a lake which is floodlit at festival times.

The buggies took us a little way back and then we transferred into a proper taxi, as the horse and trap were not allowed to cross the main road. We went to see Kim's Gun, mentioned in Rudyard Kipling's book "Kim." Its real name is Zam-Zammeh.

By now I could just afford a bag of crisps, a pot of marmalade, and some nuts, and then I was spent out.

On the way, a doctor stopped Sue and me and invited us to go for tea with him and a chat, so we got into his car and went. It was wonderful because I was terribly thirsty, not to say hungry and I just hadn't the money to buy a drink. I had to cancel breakfast, and also couldn't go to see a missionary because I hadn't the fare. I had such a good breakfast in Islamabad that I made it last until supper tonight. The doctor was a pathologist, who is going to London next month for two years.

He told us about the Pakistan and Indian war last year, and how planes came over firing on people, and his friend was injured, whilst driving him in a car. This all sounded familiar to me, having experienced war, but to him, it was all so awful, which I am sure it was. He had to operate on an Indian and another doctor wanted to amputate both legs as punishment, but this Doctor wouldn't allow it, although he said that he was sorely tempted.

I was horrified at this and said that this Indian didn't want to fire on them, any more than the

Pakistanis wanted to be fired on. I told him what I could remember of our war, and he agreed with my point of view. He took us for a ride around and then back to the Young Women's Christian Association and asked to take us out. He was an army doctor and lonely, but we had to be up early the next day so refused.

Supper was hot native food. The landlady watched us eating and enjoyed the fun when it was too hot for us!! After supper, we went to the hotel where the others were because Dorothy had kindly invited us to have a shower.

At the time we were in Pakistan, Tuesdays and Wednesdays were meatless days to conserve the meat.

Day 55   17th November

LAHORE TO AMRITSAR

From Lahore to Delhi we went on the **Grand Highway, or Great Trunk Road,** which runs through to Calcutta, it is also mentioned in Rudyard Kipling's book "Kim."

Today was a short drive to **Amritsar.** We left at 7.30 a.m. because much time was expected to be taken at the border.

We had been given a letter granting special permission to take our non-commonwealth passengers over the border. The customs official read it and said he had never seen such a letter before and could hardly believe it.

The security at the **India** border, was good, for there were three or four barriers that had to be lifted to let us through within a space of two hundred yards.

At the border, men sitting by the road were making rush mats to be used as fences and doors. The boys were eating sugar cane.

Very tall marram grass, of twelve to fifteen feet high, grew in that region, and beyond. We saw several working elephants, carrying goods, being ridden by young men. Ants ran hurriedly up and down trees.

Brightly coloured budgies, and other birds, flew from tree to tree. Mongoose hastily ran across the road, and through leaves and grasses. Large flying insects, such as I have never seen before, were swooping about the place.

The scenery along the road was quite different from what we had been used to. Ox carts slowly wended their way along, sugar cane, cotton, and wheat grew by the road.

At about 5 p.m. we arrived at Amritsar which means the Pool of Nectar. When we got off the bus there were about 200-300 children who cheered like mad and followed us down the street just like the Pied Piper of Hamlin. The streets were narrow and scruffy and full of consumptive-looking people. It was grossly overcrowded. We went to see the Golden Temple of the Sikhs.

We took off our shoes and washed our feet in the dirtiest pool imaginable. Then we entered the Holy ground, where, set in the middle of a pool, was the Golden Temple. We crossed the bridge to a building and went up and downstairs.

We strolled all around the pool and listened to music coming over a loudspeaker, interrupted by reading from the Holy Book, the Grant Sahib. We went into the Temple. Some people were sitting around singing to drumbeats, whilst other people placed coloured garlands on the ground.

This was impressive, but we could not appreciate it fully because the sun was setting and the moon was coming up, so the light was not particularly good.

There were no beggars as Sikhs are not allowed to beg, so in the Temple grounds, there are kitchens to feed the poor. Women and children sat around with their bowls of food.

In another building, a man was exhibiting war weapons that had been used in the past. People chanted with him and cheered at the end.

On coming back to the bus the throng awaited us and cheered us off.

The guest house at Amritsar was quaint. We were billeted in rooms, called "The Busy Bee," and "The Den." Beds were set in corners, nooks, and crannies, and we ate outside in the courtyard at tables beside fires. This was really great, and the food was tremendous.

In order to ration and save food, two days a week is flourless, so no bread and pastries can be bought. Another is meatless, and another rice less.

Day 56   18th November

AMRITSAR TO DELHI

Breakfast was taken out in the courtyard. It was good, with plenty to eat. Boarding the bus, we went off on the Highway again. The road was the same as the two previous days, with impressive scenes of wildlife. Budgies eating together with pigeons. Vultures standing waiting eagerly for death to strike. Squirrels scampering up trees. Camels trudging along, together with the oxen.

We crossed rivers that are tributaries to the Indus, and also crossed the Beas River, which was the further most point of Alexander the Great's expedition in Asia. Here his troops mutinied and refused to go on into unknown lands. This Grand Highway, although now modernised, is the same route that has been used for hundreds of years, between Kabul and Delhi,

Delhi was a mail stop, which made everyone eager to get there. When we got off the bus, and while Sue and Martin were hotel hunting, Barry got talking to two Indian student boys who offered to meet us the next day and show us around.

Sue, Dot, Barry, Martin, and I took one large room in a hotel. It was the only place we could get, without camping, and we didn't fancy camping for four nights, especially with Dak Houses to come next week. Anyway, the hotel put a screen down the room to divide it and the room was so long and lovely that we could have rolled up the carpet and had a dance. In it was a bathroom with hot water, seats, settee, table, and chairs. It was sheer luxury.

WEEK NINE

Day 57   19th November

DELHI

Breakfast was served in a room with soft lights, below ground level. It was approached down a red-carpeted stairway, and it was the sort of place to have evening meals and not breakfast, it nearly sent me to sleep. The boys met us at 10 am and we went to the Tourist Bureau and the American Express.

Sometime before, Barry and Martin had asked me to travel with them after Bombay. They thought I would be safer with them than travelling on my own. It was truly kind of them, but they were going to Cambodia and Vietnam. There was a war in Vietnam, and I did not want to go where there was war.

Other people on the bus, too, suggested I travel with them, but I really wanted to travel alone, as a challenge for myself, to see if I could do it. I had thought of going to north India, Nepal, Thailand, and down the Malay peninsula.

Delhi was the place to get visas, so I visited a few to see which I could get, and this would be the deciding criteria. I left the others and went to the Nepal Embassy. Several people were standing around waiting. I got my visa, while I waited and felt pleased because some other people had to leave their passports for a couple of days.

While I was there, a man who issued visas in the Burmese Embassy came in and was chatting to me. He said that if I went there for my visa, and saw him, he would get it through quickly for me. An American lady and her daughter got into conversation with me. They were on a month's holiday flying round the world. They were thrilled about my trip, left me their name and address, and invited me to stay with them because they wanted to know how the rest of my travels went. How kind of them.

From here I caught a taxi to the Cambodian Embassy but found it closed, so went on up to find the Foreigners Registry Office, to get a permit for Darjeeling. The place marked on the map happened to be a police station. I caught a scooter taxi to the right place. On the way it broke down, so out came spanners and tools. I eventually got the permit and was told that this was necessary as Darjeeling was a restricted area, owing to the war with China four years ago.

A man there, from Afghan airlines, gave me a lift back to the British Overseas Airways Corporation [BOAC] on his scooter, and asked to take me out, but I didn't want to go and hadn't time anyway, so declined.

From BOAC I got a taxi and went to visit Mr and Mrs Duff, who are missionaries with Echoes, they have been out there 19 years. They gave me a warm reception and I spent two lovely hours talking with them. I had tea and some gorgeous biscuits, which Mrs Duff had just made.

Today showed me wonderfully, how God was caring for me, by providing me with food and by making it so easy and simple for me to get my visas. It was a Day of Miracles.

It was 7 p.m. and the others had returned with a ticket for me to go to the pictures with them. First, we went for a Chinese meal in our hotel, which delicious. Then we went to the pictures for a programme that started at 10 p.m. and finished at 1.30 a.m.

It was an Indian suspense film, preceded by a documentary in English, telling the Indians how to improve their country. They had to be self-reliant and have self-respect, to increase the productivity of India, to get it on its feet. Machinery was to replace manpower, and everyone had to work hard.

Day 58   20th November

DELHI

This morning we went by the local tourist bone shaker bus to **Agra.** All of us five sat in the back and got bounced up and off the seat so much, that we yelled with pain. We hadn't gone far, when nearly all my hairpins had fallen out, through vibration. The journey was 130 miles. but was well worth the jogging ride.

We visited a tomb carved out of sandstone, then went for lunch in a hotel. While we waited for it to be served, we were entertained by a fantastically clever conjurer.

Next, we went to the Taj Mahal. It was just how I imagined. It was an awe-inspiring, beautiful piece of handiwork, built by Shahjahan in memory of his wife, and was easily the best monument we have visited on the whole trip. Calm and serene, its white marble glowed in the sunlight. Together with several people wearing beautiful, coloured saris, we walked beside the long lake of water, which reflected the entire building.

Ascending the Taj Mahal steps, we entered. It was cool and quiet. Flowers, leaves, and bees were carved out, by hand, on marble slabs, and some marble was carved to form filigree partitions. Inside were tombs. A man called out, for us to hear the echo that rang round the dome for fifteen seconds. Downstairs were two more tombs. When a torch was lit at one side, it shone through the white marble. Precious stones were inlaid in marble, to form floral arrangements

Kanchipuram was a small village close by and was a sharp contrast to the Taj Mahal. People wore bright yellow garments. Houses were long single-story dwellings with thatch rooves. Some beds stood outside, to air, in the sunshine.

From here we visited the deserted city of **Fatehpur Sikri,** built in the 16th century by Akbar the Great, where the kings have dwelt. In the courtyard, a pachisi board was laid out in the form of a cross. The emperor would have sat in the centre, on a raised stone seat. His slave girls, who were the players, were divided into two teams of eight. Each team had a different colour. They moved according to the throw of the dice.

It was deserted within twenty years by the royal court, and its red sandstone buildings have remained perfectly preserved. Tombs formed part of the dwellings, and our shoes had to be taken off. Little children kept trying to be guides, to get us to give them money, at least they were trying to earn it, also a man was going to jump from a high wall for money, but it was extremely dangerous so we wouldn't let him do it.

The ride back to Delhi was joyous because we sang most of the way, and also, I moved further down the bus, away from the bumps. Suddenly, a small bat flew in the bus and caused havoc amongst screaming girls, until it was removed. We arrived back about 10 p.m. and went for a meal nearby.

Day 59   21st November

DELHI

Postcard home on 21st November said, "India is a marvellous place, and Delhi is beautiful. The trip is almost over, but what a fabulous time we've had. It has been really great and well worthwhile."

I went to the BOAC, then the Thailand embassy. Here I got my visa with no trouble. A man from Indiaman was there and he was going to the Cambodian Embassy, so I waited for him, as I did, so the Thai people refused him a visa, until he had the Cambodian visa in his passport. I didn't have to have this first.

We shared a taxi to the Cambodian embassy and found that an air ticket had to be produced before a visa was issued. He had a right set to, and I got mine with little effort. It just turned out that if a person wanted a Transit visa, it cost 10 rupees, and took one day to obtain, and an air ticket had to be shown, whereas, for a tourist visa it was issued on the spot and cost 30.50 rupees, and no ticket was required.   Flight is the only acceptable means of transport over the border.

After getting my visas, I went back to the hotel and met Barry, who took me round to find the others in the silk shop. Of course, I could not resist such temptation, and it was so distressing, looking at so many different silks, and not knowing which to buy. At last, everyone was happy, and Barry and I nearly ended up with blouse material for me and pyjama material for him, to match. From here, we went for a snack and then back to the hotel to prepare for going out for tea with the boys to their home.

We walked along some dark, back streets to their house. We entered by an ever-open front door, from the pavement, straight into their five-foot square kitchen.

Then went into a ten-foot square room which was the only other room of the house, where the family lived in the day and slept in at night. They all lived in one room. This was neat and tidy and had a table, chairs, and couches, as well as seven calendars on the walls. They all slept and lived in one room.

There was a small yard at the back. Mother sat in a recess, cross-legged on the floor, silently cooking exciting bits and pieces for our tea. She never spoke, not even when her dignified husband came in, but quietly set his tea and food before him, without a word, and went back to her place in the kitchen. Never once did she come out to join us. India is a man's world.

Their great wild Alsatian dog kept taking every available opportunity to bound through the curtain dividing the outhouse from the living room, to invade us with full force. Such a terrifying experience, especially when we learned that he would bite. After the conversation, over tea, with the boys who were cousins, and the old gentleman, who was a scholar and taught Sanskrit, we departed.

Just up the street was the sports field, and as the boys were athletes, we went in to see the ground, and to talk to the chaps. One fellow held a world title for sprinting and he and another are to run in the Asian Games at Bangkok while I am there. From here we went back and waited for Dorothy's sari to arrive. We waited and waited, but still no sari, then after a long while it came, and what excitement. It looked terrific. So at midnight Martin, Barry Dot and I went out for coffee to celebrate. This was OK until we saw a mouse run across the restaurant floor.

Day 60   22nd November

DELHI TO JAIPUR

The two boys arrived at 7 a.m. to see us off, so came for breakfast with us. When all farewells had been said, and one of them promised to meet me at the airport when I return to Delhi, we were off, and how much we appreciate our good old Penn bus, after the joggy ride, or spine-splitter, to Agra.

Today took us through Rajasthan to **Jaipur** where monkeys hopped across rooves and swung from trees, clambered up pink stone buildings, and seemed to stand on the top laughing.

In Jaipur, we saw the Palace of the Winds. A tall tiered pink building that tiers up like a wedding cake. We just had time to make a hasty visit to a museum, where models of national costume and national dancers stood in cabinets. I found this a fascinating place. Upstairs were miniatures, dolls, natural history museum, mummies, and a skeleton about one-foot long.

Next, we went to the Astronomers Garden to an observatory and saw geometrical structures corresponding with the signs of the zodiac. All very impressive, but far beyond my comprehension or reasoning.

Today's highlight was a visit to the Amber Palace of Jaipur, which is a Fort built of red sandstone and marble. We bypassed stopping at a game reserve for this, so I'm glad it was good. Set high on a hill it could be approached on foot, or an elephant, but as an elephant cost too much we walked. It was fantastic. The view was superb, looking down across the river to the hills beyond, and down on the roof gardens, which were neglected.

In the palace, were some of the finest inlaid panels and mirror work in India. Tiny mirrors were set into walls and roofs so that when the doors were shut, and the candles were lit, they flickered and sparkled into a million pieces. Leaded light windows contrasted beautifully and blended perfectly into the mirrors. It looked enchanting.

Wandering up into turrets and down into courtyards, through many corridors, I got completely lost, it was so much like a maze. The Raja had a dozen wives who each had a separate dwelling. He had one queen and she had a bigger room.

At Jaipur, we passed a wedding. A merry throng went along, in a horse-drawn cart, to the strains of a beat-type band. They were gaily dressed, carrying gifts and flowers on their heads. These costumes of the Rajasthan are among India's most colourful.

On the way today, we saw oxen ploughing the field, with men following, sowing seed by hand. This, together, with the gross wastage of land, shows how primitive India's farming methods are. I noticed another ox cart transporting a few men. There was a camel trudging round and round, working a water wheel, and oxen drawing water from a well. We camped in the Kyser-I-Hind Hotel and salesmen were selling carving and precious stones here.

Day 61   23rd November

JAIPUR TO INDORE

Today we continued on through the very colourful, beautiful area of Madhya Pradesh. It boasts some of the most luxuriant forests, which are rich in wildlife. We never saw the animals as they are usually only seen at dusk. Much of the countryside was like the English parklands, with bushes, sparsely billeted over the rolling hills.

As we approached **Indore**, we noticed small oil lamps decking most of the house windowsills, and shop verandas. Bonfires were numerous, and fireworks were being let off in abundance. It was Diwali, the Hindu New Year. When the goddess of wealth and prosperity comes, she bypasses unlit homes.

People wear new clothes, visit one another and exchange presents. We saw some groups of people dancing to drumbeats, led by wild-looking characters, one to each group, who wore peacock feather headgear and faces were painted. They looked evil.

We slept at the circuit house. Everyone dined together at a long table. We camped on the floor, where Annett saw a white rat, in the night, in our room.

Day 62   24th   November

INDORE TO AJANTA

Today was much the same as yesterday. People of this area, wear exceptionally bright clothing and love having their photos taken.

Today we picnicked, but to do so, stopped in villages to buy food. Here the people wore rings and studs in the nose, rings on the feet, and bangles on ankles and arms. Crowds gathered around, whenever we stopped and gazed in absolute fascination and wonderment. This often happens to us when we stop in out-of-the-way places.

This was market day, and Indian men and women squatted by the roadside displaying their wares, such as fruit, clothing, material, and jewellery. Cheap jewellery, but very gay and gaudy, was a great attraction.

I have noticed much about the Indian way of life, as we have gone from village to village and passed through the countryside. Women washed clothes in the river and laid them out to dry in the sun. The thing that has struck me most, is the backwardness, due to lack of education. For instance, farming machinery seems to be almost unheard of.

A farmer will diligently walk his two oxen, pulling a wooden plough, up and down the small field, and every time they turn round, he has to walk up to them, from the back of the plough, and shout at them and beat them. After this, which takes at least one or two minutes, the beasts turn round to walk back, but in so doing churn the ground over at the end and undo the good they have done.

The plough is invariably followed by at least one person, who throws seed by hand over the ploughed land, but at the two ends, with the upheaval of land that takes place, when the oxen turn, much seed must be lost. Once I saw a tractor ploughing the field, and this seemed to be very advanced farming for India, but there, following behind it, were six people sowing seed. What a waste of manpower.

The land is partitioned off into small areas, for instance, a father will divide his land amongst his sons, and strips of unused land lie between each section, and also between the ploughed land and the road, therefore much land is wasted which could be cultivated. The area appeared fertile enough, but this was after the monsoons, and so looked better, but in the hands of people who resent machinery, it is wasted, and many crops that could be grown, are not.

A couple of oxen are used to draw water from a well, under the supervision of a man. They walk slowly up a ramp until the bucket appears, and then turn round, and walk back to let it into the ground again. One machine could be used for all this. Camels grind corn, walking round and round all day, with a man there to hasten them up.

There was no sign of famine in this area, in fact, there appeared to be a flux of bananas, oranges, tangerines, custard apples, but we were in the areas of two of India's greatest rivers, the Narmada and Tapti.

We went to **Ajanta** and camped on the veranda amongst a million midgets and ate buffet food, which was very good.

Day 63   25th   November

AJANTA

This morning we left at about 8.30 a.m., which was
nice after our earlier starts, and went with the guide to
Ajanta caves. We were not sure what to expect and
thinking they would be cold inside, took coats, only to
find that at 9 a.m. in the morning the sun was blazing,
and the caves were like ovens.

There were around thirty caves that contained
Buddhist paintings and carvings hewn out with chisel
and hammer. These told the whole historical evolution
of Buddhism in India. In one was a figure of Buddha,
and when a light was shone from one side, he looked
sad, from the other side he smiled, and from the centre
he was serious. It was fascinating. The paintings were
old but were restored and colourful. The guide knew a
lot about the stories depicted, but he was difficult to
understand.

From here we drove 90 miles to the Ellora caves,
with a picnic stop on the way. These picnic stops were
so refreshing and enjoyable, after some of the old
dumps of villages where we had stopped.

The Ellora caves, we all agreed, were preferable to
the Ajanta caves, but this was aided by the good guide,
who told us a lot about the Hindu, Jain, and Buddhist
religions. These caves, too, were carved out by chisel
and hammer, and his must have been a very laborious
task. In India, there are many such caves.

At Ellora, the Hindu cave was wonderfully carved,
and one building stood in the centre, completely carved
out of the rock, so that only the sky was above it, with
figures carved in the surrounding walls, overhung by
sheer rock. The Hindu people worship every living

creature and do not kill anything, every live thing is worshipped as the handiwork of God.

The Buddhist cave consisted of Buddha seated in an auditorium. The acoustics here were good; the slightest sound rang around the building.

This dark hollow structure was spoilt for me, by the fact that bats were hanging from the roof, and one flew at Penny and bit her. The Jain caves, which were a mile away from the others, were small, and inside Buddha sat crossed-legged and looking very fat with a potbelly. This was supposed to be the tree god and depicted plenty, therefore the god of plenty.

From the caves we went to our very last Rest House before Bombay, and what a panoramic view we had. The Rest House was set high on a hill overlooking an extremely flat plain below. The sunset was amazing. The almost full moon was tremendous, awe-inspiring, and provided such a beautiful memory for our last night of the trip.

The actual rest house, although nicely situated, was scruffy. The food was inadequate, and rice tasted peculiar so that no one ate it. The room where we put up our camp beds was crawling alive with mice, cockroaches, lizards, and ants. It was funny to watch the ants because they congregated together in groups, but when we put down some Keating's powder, they scarpered, but later lay dead like a battlefield.

To add to our joys of his place, all the electric lights went off, and we were provided with big old oil lamps, which were so top-heavy, that they were dangerous to move, and so were not much use to us.

Day 64   26th November

AJANTA TO BOMBAY

This morning dawned dull and cloudy, and we were all set for a cold last day. We left at about 7.30 a.m. to allow for heavy traffic in Bombay. The scenery was superb, as we went down, and down through the table top mountains, to the humid plains of Bombay. Never before have I seen such unusual shaped mountains. Some were conical, and others flat, just as if they had been carved, but I expect it is due to weather erosion.

Lunch stop was taken at a quiet wayside place, but suddenly, an old bull came roaring up the hill, took one look at us, and walked off, looking disgusted with picnickers.

Towards Bombay, it got hotter, and hotter, although the sky was still overcast. Humidity was high, and by the time we arrived, everyone was wet with heat, because the air is too damp to evaporate perspiration. Just outside Bombay, great iron water pipes lay on the surface by the road. These took water to the town. Rains had failed so there was a water restriction, and in parts of Bombay, water was cut off, because of the shortage.

We stayed at the Salvation Army and water was only available in the mornings, so when we went out and got hot and sticky when we came home, we couldn't wash, or wash our clothes, because the water was turned off. Full board here of bed, breakfast, lunch, tea, and supper were 12/6 per day. The place was run by a Yorkshire man, married to a Finnish lady. After we were fitted into dormitories, we had tea. My room was three floors up, and it nearly killed me carrying up all my accumulated luggage.

At teatime, I sat at a table with an English university fellow who is studying in Bombay for a year. After tea, Annette and I went to the BOAC to see if my flight had been confirmed, but the only ones that Delhi had confirmed with them were the ones I had already confirmed. Would you believe it!!

After supper, Valarie, Audrey, and I went to find the chapel. This was in a dingy back street. It was a long walk from the Salvation Army. On the way back, an Indian lady invited us for coffee, in her home. She lived at the top of a murky block of flats. Up we went, upstairs, past people lying in the doorway, up flights of dark wooden stairs, until we eventually came to her abode. The door was opened by "Daddy," who was a toothless, undernourished, pale chap from New Zealand, with an Indian accent. She was overpoweringly hospitable, and ordered the servants to bring us coffee, showed us her flat, which is worth £7,500, woke up her son to see us, gave us nuts and sweets, showed us the dog, and eventually gave me a lucky ring. She said I looked like her cousin.

Well, we were so overpowered, it seemed as if there was a catch in it somewhere. Then there was a banging on a door in the house as if someone was trying to get out of a room. The little girl went over to the door and spoke to the person banging inside, but her mother told her to come away and leave auntie alone. This was strange to us, especially as Roger had shown us the road where the "cages" are. This street is full of prostitutes, and white women for sale, from the age of eight upwards, and we began to wonder if we were the next candidates for the cages.

Anyway, we made our excuses and went to go, but "Daddy" very kindly took us back. This Indian woman kept saying how lonely she was, and how she wanted to live in England, but couldn't take the money out of the country. The only thing she could do was to get English people to take it, but I couldn't understand how.

Bombay was the final destination of our journey. I was really tired at the end of nine weeks' travel, and Bombay was so hot. Eventually, everyone went their own ways. Most stayed a few more days in Bombay. Frank flew back to England. Gill went back to England on a boat. Anastasia went to America. Someone went to Africa. Martin and Barry went off together to Cambodia and Vietnam. Some people stayed in India, and most went on the "Arcadia" to Australia and New Zealand, and I took my rout.

Day 65   27th November

BOMBAY

Today I went by taxi to the chapel meeting. I felt conspicuous, sat in amongst all the ladies' wearing saris. The place had an atmosphere of quiet strength, sincerity, and lack of frivolity about it. The service lasted two hours and one verse that was read struck me, it was about the Prodigal son, "and after he had spent all, he began to be in want, as there was a famine in the land," and I thought that would be me soon, especially as at home they said I was the prodigal daughter.

After the service, I was walking up the road and asked two people from the meeting the way to the BOAC office, and they were new to town but asked another man from the meeting who was just getting a taxi, he told me to jump in as they were passing that way and would take me. It turned out that his name was Mr French and came from Great Yarmouth, his mother who is 74 was baptized at the Lowestoft assembly about two years ago, and then his father was converted just before he died. This fellow is married to an Indian lady, and they invited me to dinner.

We went into the BOAC office, and it was so cool, because of air conditioning, that when we stepped out again it was like opening an oven door and stepping into a damp, hot, sticky atmosphere.

We went up to their flat by taxi, as they didn't have a car. Cars in India are difficult to get hold of because of the long waiting list of 3 years, and then because the price is very much higher than in the UK. If cars are purchased in the UK and taken into India the import tax is tremendous, and out of all proportion. So overall it is cheaper to hire taxis.

The French family was genuinely nice, and Mrs French was particularly hospitable. They had three children. Indian people all seem to move in together and each family has one room in the house. Seated at the large round wooden table were no less than eleven people, and this was considered a small amount for the day, as everybody was not present.

Very kindly the cook had been instructed not to make the food too hot for me, but even so, I found the curry hot and spicy although extremely nice and palatable. Different areas of India make different curries, but to me, they all tasted alike, that is hot. When eating hot curry, the best thing to eat to take the heat away is rice or bread, but not water, as this only makes the spicy fatty particles congeal and stick to the back of the throat and cause even more discomfort and pain.

After a leisurely dinner, sitting under the cool fans, Mr and Mrs French and the children decided to take me by taxi to see some of the sights of Bombay. I did so enjoy this, as we visited the exclusive areas, this was so pleasant for me because I usually have the unfortunate knack of only discovering the poor or bad areas of a town when left to wander on my own.

First, we went to the Hanging Gardens, where the sea could be seen on both sides of this narrow peninsular. Gardens were laid out neatly and people were allowed to walk on the grass, which surprised me considering the lack of rain and wear and tear on the grass. Hedges were cut into animal shapes and Indian animals at that, tigers, elephants, dogs, and peacocks.

Many multi-storied flats are being constructed in Bombay down by the coast to use every piece of ground, but this is spoiling the beauty, particularly from this point, and blocking grand sea views from older houses. This has happened in the case of the French family.

Looking up into the sky I noticed many, many vultures gliding and hovering on the wing. On enquiring the reason for this I was informed that this was a Parsee burial ground. The Parsee people leave their dead to the vultures, the Buddhists bury or entomb, whilst the Hindus cremate their dead.

Getting back into the taxi and driving further we passed a small procession of men, headed by a jaunty band, but on looking closer I saw that they were carrying a stretcher on which lay a corpse, not even covered over. The mourners looked sad, although not by hearing the music, would one detect this because when I first heard it, I thought it was a wedding. In this religion, there is no hope of being reunited with people in death, so they have cause to be sad. "If in this life only, we have hope, we are of all men most miserable."

We hadn't gone much further when we came across another type of Procession. This time it was a woman who was the centre of attraction. On enquiring about this, we were told that this woman was demon-possessed and was being led down to the sea to be bathed, and a ritual was going to take place here, also a band was in the procession. A bit further on we passed another funeral. No women are allowed to attend a Hindu funeral.

We drove out of Bombay about eighteen miles to a beach called Juhu beach, where the hotel Sun an' Sand stood. This was a luxury hotel set way back from the main highway, amongst tropical trees, and was approached along a most uninviting narrow jungle lane, but once there, what luxury! A swimming pool and beautiful sandy beach that claims to be one of the best in India. We sat in the grounds at canopied tables and drank coffee ice float, which is a coffee milkshake with ice cream. Unfortunately, we couldn't sit here long basking in the humid heat, as we had to dash back to the chapel.

Once back at the flat I was invited to have a quick shower, which I managed in about 5 minutes flat, and it was great because at the Red Shield Hostel water is turned off after first thing in the morning, to save water. Only certain areas of Bombay have a 24-hour water supply, and these include hotels and expensive areas. Then gulping down a quick cold ginger squash, Mr French and I shot off in the taxi to chapel. Despite my impression of the place, he thought it was passing through a bad spell. I sat with a lady missionary from Australia who was waiting in Bombay to catch the "Arcadia."

In the assembly, men and women sit separately. Martin arrived, one of the Pen tour boys, with his friend, who was over from the states with the Literary Evangelism Scheme. This scheme sends young people to mission stations, to sell gospel literature, to help with the work there, and with the hopes that some may take up the work permanently. I went back to the hostel with Martin in his friend's car.

After supper, Valerie and I went once more to the BOAC, but they still hadn't confirmation of my flights. I was tired of their inefficiency by now after a fortnight waiting. From here we caught a taxi to visit Frank the driver, to bid him farewell, as he was due to fly the next day. Walking back from here, down the streets, we saw several rats and mice scuttling about, around bodies lying on the pavement for the night.

Day 66   Monday 28th November

BOMBAY

Today I spent making inquiries about things. I went to Cooks with Gill, to see about trains from Calcutta to Darjeeling. After this, feeling thoroughly dissatisfied about my air ticket not being confirmed, and feeling very apprehensive about going on my own for the remainder of the trip without confirmed bookings, in case I got stranded somewhere, I went to enquire at P&O about getting on the ship. They said that they wouldn't know until tomorrow afternoon. Later I got my flights confirmed and decided not to change to ship, as I would regret not seeing all the places on my itinerary, although I could dearly do with the rest on the ship.

We idled about the shops, and then, at sunset Eva, Valerie, Frances, Audrey, and I went on one of the most impressionable trips of the whole tour. It only lasted less than half an hour and cost 3d, but it was a trip on an old sailing vessel to see the sunset over the harbour, with the Gateway of India, silhouetted against the brilliant fading sky.

It glided out and glided back. There was no noise, only the lapping of gentle water against the boat, and the slow creaking of the mast and the flap of wind in the sail. A young boy climbed up the tall mast to release the sail and at the end of the trip climbed back up to secure it again, while an older man stood at the back calling instructions and steering the ship.

On the way, I saw an atomic power station being built and a sailing boat piled high with hay. A contrast of ancient and modern.

Back at the hostel, Malcolm, Dot and Susanne arrived forlorn and sad because they had just been to see Martin and Barry off on the train. Malcolm is a sensitive boy and saying farewell upsets him. So trying to cheer them up I suggested we went out to the shops before going to bed. I bought beetle nuts with ivory carved animals inside, and a moonstone for 6/- or 7/-

postcard 28 November 1966 Bombay

Dear Mum and Dad, we've made it!! I'm actually here. Isn't it wonderful? After 9 whole weeks of travel, suspense, fun and interest we're at our destination. For me now, the fun begins. I hope I don't get lost in a jungle or cut off by an avalanche. Last Sunday I had Indian curry at the house of a brethren family and the house was full of Indian relatives, then they took me sightseeing, it was great fun. Love from Elizabeth

Day 67   Tuesday 29th November

BOMBAY

This morning Valerie, Frances, Audrey, Eva, and I went on a motorboat to visit the Elephanta Caves. These were Buddhist caves similar to Ellora and Ajanta. The guide was the best yet and explained things fully about this religion, and the different stanzas, and postures of the carvings. Buddha stood erectly, facing the main entrance, and women came with their water pots, to draw water from the pool beside Buddha.

Another girl on the boat had come by Indiaman and asked me to tour India with her, I was half tempted to, and then Valarie said I should go with her and Frances. This to me seemed a sensible thing to do, we could all four travel together and see the whole of India and Ceylon, but then I would never get home and I did promise to go back next summer. Also the longer I stayed in a country the more money I'd spend and then I'd have to stop to get a job and save up to continue my trip, and jobs in these eastern countries are very poorly paid, indeed, as well as every country is worthy of a longer visit, and no one can ever see everything there is to see, even, if he lives there a lifetime.

India is so beautiful, and so captivating, that I would simply love to have stayed longer and to satisfy my curiosity to see the south, to see how it compares with the north.

We sat and drank Mango juice, my favourite drink, and chatted, watching the monkeys rustling through the leaves on the ground, and then went back to the boat. Children followed us calling out "Buck shish," even little ragged toddlers that could hardly speak, knew how to say this word, and they gaily trotted up to us, pulling at our clothes, begging for money.

This is what they have been trained to do and therefore think is right. When children make some attempt at earning what they ask for, I don't mind so much, such as, hailing taxis, carrying bags, but even these get tiresome, because there are so many, but when I see children begging I foresee that they are going to grow into adults, such as India abounds with, and I remember the words of that film I saw in Delhi, "Self-respect, Self-restraint, and independence". This nation can never be strong while it depends so much on others, and does nothing for itself, Of course, sick, and maimed beggars are different because they don't appear to have any other means of support.

On the boat back we met a boy who is sailing tomorrow on a ship to Ceylon, and he reckoned that there was space for us, so we decided that we'd find out and go, but in the afternoon, none of us was able to find out anything about it, so I decided to stick to my original plans and fly, in spite of the fact that now I was feeling nervous at the thought of this journey ahead, but it was only because I was tired and weary of travelling for so long, because travelling overland under such conditions, and through difficult countries, customs, and climates can be thoroughly exhausting.

Mrs Liddell, a missionary in Bombay, phoned me yesterday and invited me to lunch today, so after the boat trip, she picked me up by car from the hostel and took me to her friend's house where she and I had lunch together. A servant waited on us and hovered about listening to every word. She was a timid woman, especially when driving because she has only been driving for one year. I couldn't help thinking how Dad would have given her some friendly advice, had he been in the car. She was pale and tired-looking and said that she has not been well since insects bit her, but feels that she must go on working, and requested our prayers for her. She orders the books for the Bible shop and is in charge of the secretarial side of this. After lunch, she took me to see the shop and what a lovely selection they have. Recently they have started to publish the books in India, after getting permission from England and America regarding copyright because this makes the books very much cheaper.

From here I took a taxi back to the hostel and had tea with Penny, as we had arranged. After tea, everyone set off in taxis to the dock. John and Stephanie Luxton very kindly offered to take one of my cases, so I took the small case through customs with them and onto the boat. This was the first time I had ever been on a large ship, and I was quite excited about it. People were milling about, boxes, trunks, and cases strew the pathway everywhere, and Indian porters were taking every opportunity now of earning "Buck shish." Taxis were not allowed into the Permit area carrying cases unless two rupees were paid for each case. When this was paid, they were only allowed to go a few yards, or else hire a porter. Talk about a money-making racket, this beats all, but still, I can't say that I blame the Indians for trying to earn money.

After everybody went through customs and had seen a doctor, they were then allowed onto the ship, provided, of course, that they could produce permits and tickets. I got on by showing my permit, which had only cost me 5/-, but once on I was not allowed off again.

Poor Susanne had her own luggage, plus cases for Barry and Martin and she had no money for a porter. She stood on the quay surrounded by baggage looking like a poor orphaned Annie. The trouble was that she couldn't take some on and then go back for others because they just wouldn't allow her to go off and on. The steward gave me 5/- to take down to her, he was a friendly Scot, and she then paid porters to bring the bags on.

I just loved looking over the ship but was surprised by its smallness. Our crowd were in first-class compartments, very nice, but the 3rd class looked rather like bare boards and bunks in comparison. There was a games deck and swimming pools but the thing that attracted me most was the writing and reading rooms and the library. I could just imagine three whole weeks of absolute leisure, just reading, writing, and lazing about in the swimming pool, but this was not to be my lot. I could have booked to go on that boat, but I didn't.

Before leaving the others on the boat in Bombay we had dinner with them. Afterwards, I had a shower, by the kind permission of Dorothy. What luxury, a shower and delicious food, and such a vast choice of menu. There was a music room and an entertainment hall where we watched a display of Indian dancing.

It was now 11 pm and time for visitors to go. So saying Goodbye to some and Cheerio to others Gill and I left the ship. We decided to see her sail. She sailed at 12.45 am, and the missionary from the Assembly was there too waving to me. I was so glad we waited, for we were the only people there to wave her off and it was so nice for her. The others had gone to bed, except John, Stephanie, and Bob.

The ship slipped out sideways to mid-channel and we waited until people became specks, and lights were little dots on the ocean. Then with a strange feeling of aloneness, with big human beings, we had known, now as miniature specks, Gill and I turned to wend our way homewards.

It was strange, but I had no feeling of sadness whatsoever at saying farewell to anyone, yet I had loved being with them all. Perhaps it was because I knew that my plane would arrive one and a half hours before the boat in Sydney, and I could watch her dock if I wanted to, and I would see them again.

I had made lots of new friends and had invitations to stay with the Aussie and New Zealand people.

On reaching the gate we were asked for gate permits, which we hadn't got, but we ignored the request to go inside and wait, and just walked on through ignoring his shouts after us. It was the early hours of the morning.

A kind young Indian chap asked to walk us home because there were no taxis, and it was dangerous for women to walk alone after dark. We were grateful for his offer, particularly as a car kept stopping and circling around, then coming back again, also another car full of men stopped and spoke to him about us, but he refused to listen to them.

The number of people sleeping on the pavement was incredible. Bodies were lying side by side all the way down the street. I would never have believed it had I not seen it myself. Some lay there all day, too ill to get up, and no one to care for them, and some were dying. Bombay had one million homeless people. So stepping over feet, and avoiding rats that were running amongst the bodies, we eventually reached the hostel about 2 am, only to find that we were locked out. Our escort called to the doorkeeper. He got up, groaned at us, but let us in.

After packing I got to bed at 2.30 a.m. and was to be up at 4.30 a.m. to catch the airport bus at 5 a.m. Mine was to be three more weeks of bargaining and haggling over prices, travelling on local buses and trains, being crammed, and jammed in corners by hordes of curious people. Mosquitoes, humidity, dust, and dirt. In fact, plain discomfort, and nerve-racking experiences and wondered if I was going to get from A to B without getting lost. All on my own

Day 68   Wednesday 30th November

Frances very kindly set her alarm and woke me up at 4.30 a.m. I hurriedly dressed, woke Gill to say "Cheerio," as she requested, and struggled down with my luggage. When I got to the gate it was locked and I couldn't get out. I could see the airport bus across the road, picking up people from the Taj Mahal Hotel. I rattled the gates and a man outside called up to the hostel doorkeeper. He came, drowsily downstairs complaining that I had not told him I was leaving early.

Eventually, I stepped out of the gate just in time to see the airport bus leave. I started walking until I found taxis, but they couldn't give me a lift because the drivers were sleeping, and no one would offer to take me. So after getting a flight booked and getting up early, now I was locked out of the hostel, and almost in despair.

I stood alone in the dark street with my luggage, wondering what would happen next.
My next adventures were just about to begin

FOOTNOTE
If you were on this bus with me, or know anyone who was, I would love you to get in touch with me.

Printed in Great Britain
by Amazon